THE ERNST & YOUNG GUIDE
TO EXPANDING IN THE GLOBAL MARKET

The Wiley/Ernst & Young Business Guide Series

The Ernst & Young Business Plan Guide
The Ernst & Young Guide To Raising Capital
The Ernst & Young Guide To Expanding in the Global Market
The Ernst & Young Resource Guide To Global Markets 1991
The Ernst & Young Management Guide To Mergers and Acquisitions

THE ERNST & YOUNG GUIDE TO EXPANDING IN THE GLOBAL MARKET

CHARLES F. VALENTINE

Ernst & Young International Trade Advisory Services
Washington, D.C.

JOHN WILEY & SONS

New York • Chichester • Brisbane • Toronto • Singapore

Library of Congress Cataloging-in-Publication Data:

Valentine, Charles F.
   The Ernst & Young guide to expanding in the global market /
Charles F. Valentine (Ernst & Young).
     p.   cm.
   Revised ed. of: The Arthur Young international business guide.
   Includes bibliographical references.
   ISBN 0-471-52830-7
   ISBN 0-471-53007-7 (pbk.)
   1. International business enterprises—Management.
2. International business enterprises—Management—Case studies.
I. Ernst & Young. II. Valentine, Charles F. Arthur Young
international business guide. III. Title. IV. Title: Ernst and
Young guide to expanding in the global market.
HD62.4.V354 1991
658.1'8—dc20   90-12588

Printed in the United States of America

91 92 10 9 8 7 6 5 4 3 2 1

CONTENTS

PART 2 THE ERNST & YOUNG FOUR-STEP
APPROACH TO GOING INTERNATIONAL   33

PREFACE

During the past ten years, the United States has imported far more goods than we have exported. Our trade deficit has swelled, and should be of concern to all Americans. The reasons given for this trade deficit vary, from misaligned exchange rates, to high interest rates caused by our budget deficit, to conspicuous consumption. One reason that has only recently been given more prominence is the action, or inaction, of individual U.S. companies themselves.

The Ernst & Young Guide to Expanding in the Global Market does not intend to address the overall issue of U.S. foreign trade deficits. Rather, this book is concerned with the following key issues:

- A small minority of U.S. companies export their products and services.

- Many more companies could succeed overseas if they would commit themselves to trying.

For the past seventeen years, I have advised U.S. companies on their efforts to do business in the lucrative and constantly growing global marketplace. My clients have entered markets throughout Europe, Asia, the Caribbean, and Latin America, often with great success. Generally speaking I've found that many U. S. companies are in a better position to beat their competitors overseas than management believes possible; however, I've also watched a lamentable number of companies go international for the wrong reasons, without much forethought or preparation. The results have been predictably dismal. If only American executives would think more carefully about the new situations they encounter overseas, they might experience less disappointment—and make more money—in countries where consumers are in far more than eager to buy American-made goods and services.

My original intention in writing *The Ernst & Young Guide to Expanding in the Global Market* was to provide an introductory guide to going international for small and medium-sized companies new-to-exporting and the global marketplace. The process is complex. No single book can describe every step and substep in detail appropriate to every single company. Yet this book offers a systematic approach that, if followed closely, can assist your company in meeting the challenge of an international venture. Doing business abroad, despite its complexities, is neither as difficult nor as dangerous as many American corporate officers believe it to be.

I was frequently asked the following questions after the publication of the first edition: "Should small and medium-size companies export? Isn't international business too complicated for small and medium size companies? If big companies dominate exports, isn't it supposed to be that way?" My answer has always been an emphatic "No!" I think we can learn a lot from our major competitors in this respect. In both Japan and Korea, government agencies and trade associations are actively encouraging small and medium-size firms to *invest overseas*. It is not even questioned there whether small and medium-size companies should be exporting. If we consider Taiwan and Hong Kong, two of the world's export power houses, we must remember that the majority of the exporters are small companies, and in fact, very small by our standards. There is no reason why small and medium-size U.S. companies cannot export with the right commitment and attitude.

I have also become increasingly aware that even larger companies with experience in international business were falling short on many accounts. These companies do not have a way to systematically evaluate and make good decisions regarding international business. Many companies, I found, may have a good understanding of a few country markets, but were sorely lacking when it came to knowledge of opportunities in other markets. Even major companies with household name recognition were weak when it came to responding to the new global market. Accordingly, in this edition we have added a number of sections which will help larger companies recognize new opportunities and evaluate their position to exploit these opportunities.

The United States now faces a new economic reality. As American business people, we have a choice. We can limit ourselves to our large but mature domestic market, a market in which foreign competitors often beat us on our own turf. Or we can reach out to the huge, growing often lucrative global marketplace where, if properly prepared, we can play the game and win. Our choice will determine our fate—certainly our fate as business people, and perhaps our fate as a nation as well.

The companion to this book, *The Ernst & Young Resource Guide to Global Markets 1991*, presents current information vital to exporters. The *Resource Guide* will be updated yearly and will offer timely data on key markets and current trends. The *Resource Guide* serves as a reference volume which will be invaluable to the practical exporter.

A NOTE REGARDING THE CASE STUDIES

All case studies in this book describe actual incidents that have occurred in actual U.S. companies entering the global marketplace In some cases, I have referred to the companies by name. In others, however, I have changed the names of the companies or their representatives. But the cases themselves exemplify real business issues and how real companies have dealt with them.

CHARLES F. VALENTINE

Washington, D.C.

ACKNOWLEDGMENTS

Like all complex endeavors, the process of writing *The Ernst & Young Guide to Expanding in the Global Market* has benefitted from the ideas, insights, and experience of many people. Although the following acknowledgments can't provide sufficient recognition to everyone who has made a contribution, I want at least to thank all those who have helped me in significant ways.

First and foremost, I want to thank my family for their patience and support during all our many years of travel, and for their valuable input into this book. I could not have reached the final goal without their help. Most of all, I want to thank my wife, Jean, who suggested the idea for the book in the first place.

I also owe deep gratitude to my colleagues at Ernst & Young. Their expertise has added much to this book; their critical comments, too, have provided valuable insights throughout the tasks of writing and editing. In particular, I would like to thank Ed Bartholomew and Mort Meyerson for their energetic work in clarifying issues in the text and for their support and enthusiasm for the project from start to finish. The new edition of this book could not have been completed without the assistance of Roger Poor and Ginger Lew, who functioned as co-authors, and Steven Graubart, and Marianna Bertucci, who helped in many ways. Each of them made significant contributions to the second edition. I would also like to thank Jim Tobin for his assistance on tax matters, and Rob McLean for his help with strategic planning issues. I also greatly appreciate Ed Bartholomew's reviewing the final manuscript on behalf of the firm.

In addition, I wish to thank the following people: Dave Nugent, selection, placement, and training of expatriate staff; Chieko Fujii and Joanna Pineda for their help in providing information on a multitude of research issues.

Many corporate officers have also made important contributions, both in their specific advice on going international and in their comments on the manuscript. I wish I could thank them all by name, for I appreciate their many kinds of help. Special thanks go to Norman St. Clair, who contributed tips for doing business overseas, and to Frank Kelly of Gerber Products Company, who provided excellent case studies and reflections on a wide variety of issues.

Jeff Brown, my editor at John Wiley & Sons, has been the ideal editor: constantly supportive yet ready with specific suggestions, comments, and ideas that have improved the manuscript in many ways. Elizabeth Doble, managing editor, has been thoughtful and efficient in seeing this book through the production process, and Northeastern Graphic Services made many insightful changes when they copy-edited the manuscript.

C.F.V.

INTRODUCTION

Consider for a moment this single fact : *Only 80,000 American companies sell their products and services abroad.*

Now reflect just briefly on the implications of this statistic. Since approximately 17.5 million firms exist in the United States, the percentage that exports is a remarkably small fraction of the total number. What about the millions of other companies? Are their products and services totally unappealing to customers in other countries? Highly improbable. Is marketing American services and goods overseas too much trouble to be worthwhile? Unlikely in an age when easy travel and instantaneous communications make the whole planet (in media theorist Marshall McLuhan's famous phrase) a global village. So why do only a small minority of American firms bother doing business abroad?

Before we answer these questions, consider a second statistic: *The U.S. trade deficit was $109.4 billion in 1989.*

Most American business people are aware of this dismal situation, and many express justified concern about its effects on the country's economic future. In his best-selling book *Iacocca* (Bantam, 1984), for instance, Chairman Lee Iacocca of Chrysler Corporation sounded the alarm: "Right now, we're in the midst of another major war with Japan. This time it's not a shooting war. . . . The current conflict is a trade war. But because our government refuses to see this war for what it really is, we're well on the road to defeat."

"Make no mistake: our economic struggle with the Japanese is critical to our future. We're up against a formidable competitor and . . . we'd be lucky to stay even with them" (p. 331).

However, blaming Japan misses the real point. The United States faces more than just one commercial adversary. "Japan, Inc." is only the most formidable of our competitors, and Japan-bashing is not the solution to our economic woes. Other nations pose dangers to American economic well-being as well. Germany, France, Italy, and other European countries are effective in their marketing efforts throughout the world. The impact of the European Community's "Project 1992" is beginning to be realized. The Four Tigers of Asia (Taiwan, Hong Kong, Singapore, and Korea) have entered global markets with consistent success, and are becoming more sophisticated in the types of products they are exporting. They are also being emulated by up-and-coming Asian countries like Thailand and Malaysia. Brazil has become an economic powerhouse, and Chile has begun to emerge as a major exporter in certain areas. The People's Republic of China, in spite of its uncertain political position, is still on its way to becoming a powerful long-term competitor. In fact, with "export led growth" now generally being accepted by economic development specialists as the best way for an economy to expand, we will be witnessing strong attempts by countries throughout the world to become major exporters.

The U.S. business community must face up to the fact that we are less experienced than many other countries in terms of international business. I am reminded of a story one of my colleagues, an international business consultant, tells me. Whenever he tells an American that he works in international business, the American is immediately fascinated, probably conjuring up in his mind images of exotic travel. Whenever he tells the same thing to a European, the European asks, "So, what kind of business do you do?" The European doesn't think twice about the term international. For him, this is an inherent and normal part of business.

Exporting plays a bigger role in other countries than in the United States. The following figure shows exports as a percentage of Gross Domestic Product (GDP) for a number of key countries and illustrates that the U.S. ranks very low by this measure of export activity.

FIGURE 1. Exports as a % of GDP 1988
Source: The World Bank

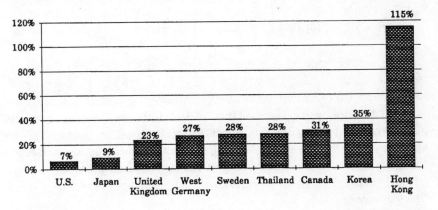

The real tragedy is that these two problems—minimal American commercial activity abroad and U.S. trade deficits—are closely related. Worse yet, they are mostly our own fault. Although regulations, tariffs, and currency fluctuations unquestionably enter into the overall picture, the weak American role in global trade cannot be blamed solely on other countries' activities. Mark H. McCormack, in *What They Don't Teach You at Harvard Business School* (Bantam, 1984), describes how we run the risk of losing the battle by default: "You can count on your fingers the American companies which are maximizing their full potential in international markets.

"Of all the world's companies, American-run businesses are by far the most arrogant and chauvinistic. Most of their international divisions haven't taken the time to break down language and cultural barriers, preferring to declare them impenetrable" (p. 83).

If McCormack's statements are true—and the evidence continues to accumulate in his favor—then American businesses are choosing to pass up opportunities of truly historic proportions. To be sure, doing business abroad is complex. It presents difficulties that often differ from those that companies have learned to address in the domestic arena. But American firms that refuse to consider the possibility of international ventures are ignoring three fundamental facts:

- The international marketplace is vast.
- Many nations are succeeding in markets where Americans once excelled.
- Financially sound companies stand to gain much from well-chosen, well-planned international ventures.

By ignoring these facts, American companies not only forfeit overseas markets but also thwart their domestic efforts. Foreign firms have not restricted themselves to local markets; on the contrary, companies of many nations regard the United States as their most profitable territory. U.S. firms, too, must widen their scope of activities to survive and prosper. The new business reality of the 1990s is that international trade, far from being a luxury available to only a few firms, is crucial for most American companies *simply to compete effectively at home.*

Will U.S. companies take advantage of the opportunities awaiting them in the global marketplace? Or will they decide that the challenge is too great, thereby relinquishing sales and profits to other countries?

Iacocca describes the possible consequences of the situation: "I don't know when we're going to wake up, but I hope it's soon. Otherwise, within a few years our economic arsenal is going to consist of little more than drive-in banks, hamburger joints, and video-game arcades" (p. 339).

A NEW MAP TO THE NEW BUSINESS LANDSCAPE

Resolution of the current U.S. trade deficit and its attendant economic ills is beyond the scope of a single book. The overall trade situation *is* significant to us here, however, because of what it implies about how Americans do business overseas, or more often how we *don't* do business overseas. Because for the most part, American companies don't bother to compete outside the domestic marketplace.

We need to ask why only 80,000 American firms export their products or services. What accounts for such a low proportion of U.S. companies in the international marketplace?

The reason is *not* a lack of interest. Thousands of American business executives want to do business abroad. For example, in 1988 alone, U.S. Department of Commerce district offices sponsored 3,249 seminars and conferences on exporting, providing assistance to 585 new-to-export firms and 2,092 new-to-market firms, and conducted 125,390 individual counseling sessions on exporting. Most American business people have begun to grasp the promise of international trade. In addition:

- *Many domestic markets have reached maturity.* If American companies are to expand, they must look overseas.

- *The United States represents for only 4 percent of the world's population.* The other 96 percent of the world's people form a vast market as yet untapped by many U.S. firms.

- *Foreign consumers are often ready—even eager—to buy American-made goods.* The label "Made in the U.S.A." gives many products special appeal overseas.

Yet despite their awareness of how promising overseas trade is, many executives hesitate to proceed with international ventures. Doing business abroad sometimes seems too complex, too confusing, and too risky. Despite all the information available, few sources of facts and advice address the full range of the American business-person's needs during the course of going international. The sporadic, often confusing array of data addressing issues of international trade often has tended to make the option of doing business abroad seem excessively risky. Many executives therefore attempt to "play it safe" by sticking to domestic ventures.

As a result, the ultimate reason for America's poor showing in the world marketplace is that most corporate officers have not understood the specific tasks necessary for success overseas. American business people have lacked a map to guide them through the international business landscape.

The Ernst & Young Guide to Expanding in the Global Market now provides that map.

ORGANIZATION OF THE BOOK

In this edition, we have added a number of new sections. The book is organized as follows:

Parts 1 and 2 are written with the new-to-export company in mind. Part 1 provides an analysis of why companies should consider going overseas. Part 2 presents the Four Steps, an approach companies can use when first going international. While the focus of this section is the new-to-export company, we believe that there are many useful tips for international business development even for an experienced exporter. This is especially true of Step 3, regarding a more sophisticated strategy development tool, and Step 4, which provides a number of key insights on how to effectively compete internationally.

As mentioned above, Step 3 of Part 2 presents the Global Strategic Positioning Cube. This is a tool we have developed for analyzing a company's strategic position and for identifying those actions which should be taken to improve its position. The Cube is primarily relevant for those companies that have already demonstrated commitment to international activity.

Part 3 presents a few selected examples of companies that have been successful in going international. These have been selected to show that even small companies can succeed in global markets.

Part 4 presents a number of observations regarding the state of U.S. international business activity. These are insights into the "export mentality" of U.S. business, and specific challenges that must be met are also presented.

The Ernst & Young Guide to Expanding in the Global Market, as outlined above, contains material which helps companies in the *process* of international market development; this is information which will not become outdated. This edition of the book is accompanied by a reference volume containing information about key trends and key markets which will need periodic updating. *The Ernst & Young*

Resource Guide to Global Markets, 1991, includes information on salient international issues and trends, regional and country data, and assorted reference material including key public sector contacts.

THE FOUR STEPS

This book offers a systematic approach to determining whether your company should consider undertaking an international venture, and—in case the answer is yes—the book also provides an overview of the tasks necessary for planning and executing the venture itself. The Ernst & Young four steps are:

1. Testing the waters
2. Learning the language
3. Mapping out a strategy
4. Beating the competition at its own game

After an initial chapter that provides a brief sketch of the global marketplace, each of the four steps of this approach is explained in detail.

Step 1: Testing the Waters

The first step is to test the waters—that is, to evaluate your company's financial and organizational readiness for international ventures. Step 1 explains how to

- determine your company's state of readiness,
- acquire preliminary background information about foreign markets,
- establish possible target markets,
- identify potential windows of opportunity,
- confirm market readiness by seeking an "instant gratification" sale,

- acquire financial assistance for further research, and
- develop an initial focus.

Step 2: Learning the Language

International trade uses a "language" of international conditions and business practices that differs from the language most Americans understand. Since foreign business competitors will be anticipating your company's arrival in their territory, you must learn their rules to have any chance for success.

Step 2 therefore provides information on how to

- develop an international perspective,
- identify and overcome obstacles,
- conduct market research,
- analyze risks,
- evaluate corporate tax issues, and
- explore available government funding programs and alternative schemes for financing.

Step 3: Mapping Out a Strategy

The key to entering a foreign market is an intelligent, well- considered strategy that addresses market structure, risk factors, legal and financial considerations, and timing, among other issues. Step 3 provides the information you need to develop a market entry strategy for your international venture. Initial discussions answer these questions:

- What is strategy?
- What are the differences between strategy and strategic management?

- Why is strategy necessary?
- What issues should a strategy address?
- What period of time should a strategy cover?
- Who should plan and implement a strategy?

After clarifying these issues, Step 3 provides a framework that can easily be adapted to your company's needs as you undertake the process of strategic management whether you are new to exporting or experienced in international operations, in which case, a new tool—"The Cube"—may be useful for further strategy development.

THE CUBE

This book presents the *Ernst & Young Global Strategic Positioning Cube* *("The Cube")*. The fact that both opportunities and threats exist on a global basis means that business decision-making has become more complex and difficult. Ernst & Young developed The Cube to assist companies already involved in international business operate in the new global environment.

The Cube is a tool that companies can use to evaluate their global strategic position. The Cube allows companies to assess their strengths and weaknesses in order to focus marketing efforts, improve their competitiveness, and to strengthen in-house capabilities. The Cube can be used to analyze a company's global position, or to compare a company's position across regions or among countries.

Step 4: Beating The Competition at Their Own Game

The final step of going international is to develop a capability for aggressive competition overseas. By selecting imaginative, adaptable expatriate staff members, training your personnel in cross-cultural issues, following several time-honored tips for success, and avoiding common pitfalls, your company can become self-sufficient in its international venture.

SUCCESS STORIES

Many U.S. companies are succeeding overseas. Some of them are large companies like IBM and Boeing that dominate their industries worldwide. Others are small firms that have found unique niches. But all of them have one thing in common: they have made an attempt to understand overseas markets and fill market needs based on that research and evaluation.

THE CHALLENGES AHEAD

The challenges of international business are clear. Companies must think in new ways about their markets and competitive threats. A new perspective must be gained on the world, and new strategies developed for the future.

The challenges ahead are many, but must begin with the decisive development of clearly defined international business objectives and the commitment of the necessary resources to meet these objectives. Ultimately, the rewards make the challenges worthwhile. I believe that U.S. businesses will demonstrate that they can meet the new realities of international opportunities and competition seriously.

Your company *can* succeed in doing business abroad.

PART 1

THE GLOBAL MARKETPLACE—
WHY AND WHEN TO REACH IT

International business is older than the ancient Phoenician traders and the trans-Asian caravans, yet only during the past century has the world become a truly global marketplace. The development of modern transportation and telecommunications technology has allowed business people in almost every nation on earth to sell their products and services to customers virtually everywhere else.

THE DECLINE AND FALL OF THE AMERICAN EMPIRE?

For most of the past four decades, the United States held a position of preeminence—if not outright dominance—in the global marketplace. American industrial productivity became the envy of the world; American distribution networks spread into almost every country; American marketing techniques achieved unprecedented effectiveness. The United States not only won the Second World War, but also established what, at least in commercial terms, proved to be an American Empire.

But now America's leadership has eroded. Several countries outstrip the United States in productivity; foreign goods often cost less than ours; other nations' marketing campaigns increasingly succeed at wooing American and foreign consumers alike. The most dramatic result of this erosion is that the U.S. trade deficit continues to remain significant. An equally disheartening consequence of this situation is more specific: individual American companies keep losing sales to foreign competitors, with harmful side effects both for corporate health and for the well-being of individual employees.

What accounts for this country's decline in commercial leadership? What has brought about the loss of American dominance in international trade?

Four commonly offered explanations for this situation are *increased materials costs, increased labor costs, trade protectionism,* and *the overvaluation of certain currencies.* Many raw materials have become steadily more expensive since the World War II era, with further increases likely as supplier nations grow more sophisticated and organized in dealing with their customers. Meanwhile, labor costs within the United States have risen as well, so that many American firms compete at a disadvantage with companies in foreign countries where wage scales are far lower. Laws and regulations in other countries have created worries about trade protectionism, and consequently about American companies' access to foreign markets. Finally, the periodic overvaluation of the U.S. dollar has made some American goods more expensive than comparable foreign products.

These factors unquestionably contribute to the problems of lost sales and trade imbalances. A couple of other factors over which we have more control, however, also make a difference—factors that are uncomfortable to face but important to accept if American companies are to regain a position of strength in the global marketplace. These factors are *cultural presumptions* and *hasty or inadequate business strategies.*

Cultural Presumptions

Beliefs, customs, traditions, and ways of doing business all vary from one country to another, and even within individual countries. No one from one culture can know all the subtleties of another. Still, the reason many U.S. businesses fail overseas is that management refuses to grasp even the *possibility* of cultural differences. Too many American business people presume that the whole world does business our way. Worse, they say as much. How often have you heard Americans speak of other nationalities in words like these?

"Back home, we wouldn't waste so much time."

Or: "I can't understand how these people get anything done at all."

Or: "What this place needs is some good old American know-how."

Case Study

Three executives from an American farm machinery corporation flew to Tokyo with hopes of selling tractors to Japanese buyers. The Americans—none of whom had traveled to Japan before—then arranged a meeting with the representatives of a large soybean company.

As far as the tractor company executives could determine, their presentation went well. The Japanese listened politely to the English sales pitch and to the subsequent translation. After an initial statement of the price of the tractors, however, the Japanese just sat there. One of the Americans therefore held forth a while longer, elaborating on points he had already made. The Japanese listened but once again said nothing. As the silence became more and more disquieting the senior American executive proposed a lower price for his company's products. Even so, the Japanese made no response. Ultimately the Americans lowered their price far lower than they had ever intended, never realizing that the Japanese executives had fallen silent not so much to show displeasure or disinterest, but simply to consider the initial proposal—all in keeping with standard Japanese practice.

People in other cultures use time, space, and language so differently from us that we often totally misread their intentions. For instance, Americans often feel uncomfortable with silence. We want a conversation to keep moving. On the other hand, the Japanese and many other nationalities prefer a less "crowded" style of verbal interaction. The American negotiators in the preceding case study assumed that their Japanese counterparts were ignoring them or brushing them off; they failed to understand that the Japanese preferred not to respond at once and needed time to ponder the situation.

The issue isn't merely linguistic. Food, clothing, and personal customs also can create vast obstacles for international business travelers to surmount or avoid. Almost everyone who has worked abroad can tell stories about mishaps and embarrassments while on assignment. The point isn't to avoid every conceivable misunderstanding or misstep. Rather, the point is to prepare yourself and your company for dealing with the new cultural rules overseas. To be unprepared is to damage your efforts—and, in some cases, to doom them altogether.

Hasty or Inadequate Business Strategies

Perhaps the most common factor contributing to lost international sales is faulty strategy. Businesses that routinely plan their domestic ventures with careful, thoughtful, long-term research and strategizing often throw caution to the wind when moving into the global marketplace. Some managers even prefer "winging it" to any kind of planning at all.

Instead of doing market research and planning a sound strategy, many American companies prefer a "U.S. Marines" approach to international ventures. Invade the foreign land! Establish a beachhead! Take the country by storm! Unfortunately, the usual result of this attitude is that companies fail miserably in their first foreign endeavor and resolve thereafter not to pursue international operations at all. "Oh, we tried going abroad once and lost our shirts," management says, "so we stick to selling where we understand the rules." The irony is that with proper forethought, research, and

Case Study

Bill Hastings, the assistant director of marketing for a small American manufacturing company, visited Bangkok to investigate the possibility of distributing the company's products in Southeast Asia. Bill traveled with Cheryl Acosta, field director for the company's international operations. Neither of them had had any prior experience in Asia. Bill, in fact, had never traveled outside the United States. Both executives felt mildly apprehensive about being neophytes in the field, but they felt great excitement, too, as if they were the first explorers in an uncharted area. (Neither acknowledged that their counterparts in other companies probably had had years of international experience and had developed a mastery of Southeast Asian business practices.)

Bill and Cheryl attempted to complete a twelve-country marketing study in six weeks. Bill figured that once he obtained the facts and made a quick decision on how to proceed, sales would start rolling in. But they found the environment baffling and made little headway. Frustrated, they impulsively recommended a plan to headquarters that ended in a fiasco one year later.

"I can't understand what happened," Bill reflected in the aftermath. "The same method worked just fine when we started operations in Los Angeles."

planning, you *can* come to understand the rules overseas. You can even use these rules to your own advantage.

THE PROMISE OF DISTANT SHORES

The fact remains: Foreign markets offer vast opportunities for American companies. The benefits in sales alone are difficult to overestimate. Other advantages include increased brand name recognition, potential product diversification, company expansion, and protection of domestic markets through more effective competition with foreign firms operating in the United States. Success in the international arena is a goal best achieved through careful planning. As such, it is a goal accessible even to small and medium-sized companies.

A survey by Dun & Bradstreet showed the optimism and potential for small and medium-size companies to develop exports. According to Joseph W. Duncan, corporate economist and chief statistician, "The conventional view is that exporting is almost exclusively a big-business activity, yet the results of our survey show that small businesses actually represent a substantial portion of all exporters. In fact, with the weaker U.S. dollar, improved foreign markets and a growing array of support programs, more and more small businesses are venturing where only the Fortune 500 have tread before." Duncan continued to say that "The hesitance of some small firms ... to export may be a function of an obstacle that exists, not in the marketplace, but in the mind of the business owner."

Any stable, healthy business should at least investigate the prospects of going international. The minimum requirements are the following:

- *An open mind.* Any international venture will bring you face to face with unfamiliar business practices; with different customs, beliefs, attitudes, expectations, and tastes; and with unaccustomed kinds of potential risk and benefit. To succeed overseas, you must set aside at least some of your assumptions about what makes sense and how to get things done.

- *Careful planning.* Commerce abroad differs from commerce at home, but the difference doesn't mean that the global marketplace is a free-for-all. Just as entering a new domestic market requires research, goal setting, and strategy, entering a foreign market requires careful planning. In a field where competitors are abundant, shrewd, and experienced, "winging it" is an invitation for disaster.

- *Aggressive, strenuous action.* When great geographical distances, cultural differences, and logistical complexities come into play, business people must act with foresight, clarity of mind, and energy. The effort involved is often considerable, but so are the potential payoffs.

Before sketching when and why companies should consider undertaking an international venture, we should have a look at the global marketplace today. An overview of world trade will provide a context for understanding what American businesses encounter when they go overseas.

Fifty or a hundred years ago, international commerce functioned in a relatively simple way. The less-developed countries sold raw materials to the industrialized nations; the industrialized nations sold finished products to each other and to the less-developed countries. Although this description oversimplifies the situation to some degree, it portrays the basic condition of the world economy before the second World War.

Since then, however, the picture has changed. Raw materials and finished goods no longer flow in the relatively simple patterns of the prewar era. Economies are now intricately interdependent.

We Own Them, They Own Us

American corporations have established foreign subsidiaries throughout the history of this country's participation in international trade. General Motors, General Electric, IBM, E. I. du Pont de Nemours, and Exxon are only a few of the biggest firms whose network of companies extends literally around the world; thousands of smaller corporations have more modest multinational operations.

Meanwhile, the United States remains a magnet for foreign capital. By 1988, direct foreign investment in U.S. companies totaled $329 billion, compared to $90 billion by 1980. U.S. direct foreign investment abroad totaled $327 billion by 1988. (Sources: *The New York Times*, May 20, 1989; *Survey of Current Business*, August 1989). *Forbes* magazine summarized the situation as follows: "If Americans sometimes lack faith in their own economy, it is quite clear that many well-heeled foreigners have a good deal of faith in it" (*Forbes*, July 28, 1986, p. 200). As a result, many companies regarded by domestic consumers as American firms are in fact partially or totally foreign-owned. For instance, Britain's Grand Metropolitan P.L.C. owns Pillsbury Company and Almaden Vineyards, Inc. Bridgestone Corporation of Japan owns Firestone Tire and Rubber Company. Switzerland's Nestlé owns Carnation and Alcon Laboratories.

A New Economic Order

Obviously, the game has changed. American companies no longer dominate the international marketplace simply by virtue of being American. Firms based in other countries can match and frequently exceed U.S. firms' performance. Foreign companies have invaded markets—including markets within the United States—that were once almost exclusively the province of American corporations. The situation has no chance of returning to the "good old days." On the contrary, the situation is growing more and more complex.

Who are the players in this drama, and what are the implications for U.S. business?

Japan.   The country that draws the most attention these days—and that inspires the most awe, fear, and anger—is, of course, Japan. With a 1988 GNP of U.S. $2.86 trillion and a 1988 trade surplus of $77.47 billion, Japan is the second largest market economy after the United States. Japan's rebirth out of the postwar ashes is one of the great success stories of modern industrialization.

During recent decades, the United States has found its former nemesis and current political ally more of a challenge than most observers once expected. America's trade deficit with Japan reached $48 billion during 1988, with the imbalance unlikely to decrease significantly in the foreseeable future. In response, prominent American spokespeople in both the public and private sectors have started calling for trade sanctions against Japan. These spokespeople assert that Japanese businesses have taken advantage of American labor costs, trade policies, and currency exchange rates to further their own goals unfairly. Yet it's surely significant that Japan maintains a surplus with most of its trading partners (see Table 1 for statistics). European nations whose exports and imports result in a trade deficit with Japan include the United Kingdom, France, West Germany, and the Netherlands. Japan also maintains a surplus in trade with South Korea, Taiwan, China, Thailand, Singapore, and Hong Kong. Clearly, if the Japanese are taking unfair advantage of the United States, they are somehow doing so as well with most other industrialized nations.

The likelier—though more painful—explanation is that Japan has developed more skillful and imaginative marketing and distribution practices than those used by other nations. The Japanese are

TABLE 1. Countries/regions with which Japan has a trade surplus
(1988 figures, in U.S. $ millions)

Country/Region	Japanese Trade Surplus
OECD Countries	93,139
United Kingdom	6,439
France	676
West Germany	7,692
Netherlands	4,057
USSR	359
Canada	1,874
United States	47,998
Developing countries, total	9,247

Source: OECD, "Monthly Statistics on Foreign Trade," June, 1989.

simply excelling at the international game that other nations started.

The European Community. Meanwhile, the European Community (EC) remains the United States' most important trading partner and one of its most powerful competitors. Founded in 1958 to promote economic integration and collaboration within Western Europe, the EC now consists of twelve member-nations: Belgium, Denmark, France, Greece, Ireland, Italy, Luxembourg, the Netherlands, Portugal, Spain, the United Kingdom, and West Germany. The EC nations had a combined GDP of $4,270 billion in 1987. The EC economies vary in their productivity and marketing sophistication; consequently, trade surpluses and deficits vary from country to country.

EC firms provide U.S. companies with some of their most energetic competition. Philips, Telefunken, and Blaupunkt, produce electronics components that American consumers covet as much as they do Japanese components. Appliance manufacturers such as Krups are now virtually household names in the United States. And European clothing companies—among which Gucci, Yves St. Laurent, Benetton, and Giorgio Armani are only four of the most prominent—now draw customers worldwide. In short, the EC countries, though varied in their business practices and industrial productivity, challenge the United States as much as Japan does.

The Newly Industrialized Countries.   Japan and Europe are only part of the picture. Just as the United States once felt confident of its commercial supremacy only to face the challenge of Japanese and European competitors, now all the developed nations face new pressure from the newly industrialized countries (NICs). Taiwan, South Korea, and Singapore have now attained sufficient industrial prowess to compete in the global marketplace. Brazil—the fifth largest nation in land area and the sixth largest in population—has made striking advances in recent decades. Malaysia, and Thailand are poised to present a challenge as well in the decade of the 1990s.

The People's Republic of China.   Meanwhile, the People's Republic of China (PRC) is the sleeping giant of international trade. With a population of over one billion and with vast natural resources (including coal and oil reserves, minerals, waterpower, and arable land), the PRC will some day present all other nations with a formidable trading competitor.

Future Contenders.   Thailand, Malaysia; the Philippines, Indonesia, and some of the newly freed Eastern Bloc countries are becoming more economically active and will continue to do so in the future. Variables influencing their development will include the state of the global economy, the cost of oil and other resources, political stability, and currency fluctuations.

Figures 2 and 3 show U.S. exports and imports by destination for 1988. Further U.S. trade data are provided in *The Ernst & Young Resource Guide to Global Markets, 1991.*

New Challenges, New Opportunities

The United States, Europe, and even Japan can no longer assume a right to commercial supremacy by default. Other countries will join the ranks of the industrialized nations. Some of these nations will achieve leadership in trade through good strategy, hard work, and persistence. Whether the United States maintains its tradition of excellence in both industry and trade depends largely on how well

FIGURE 2. U.S. Exports 1988, Total $316 Billion
(Source: U.S. Department of Commerce)

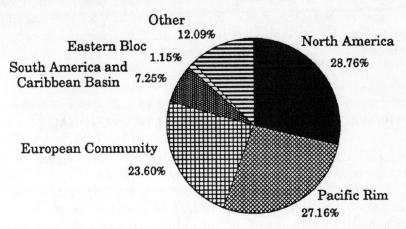

and how imaginatively American companies take up the challenge before them.

To summarize: The global marketplace offers both great challenges and great opportunities. Competitors are numerous and often sophisticated, yet the potential benefits of international ventures may outweigh the risks.

FIGURE 3. U.S. Imports 1988, Total $442 Billion
(Source: U.S. Department of Commerce)

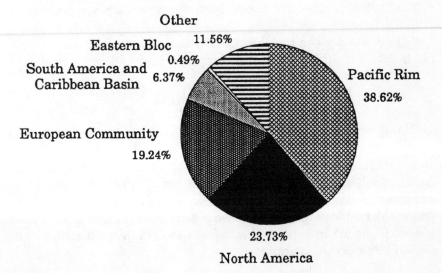

Having briefly sketched the global marketplace, we now address the question of when a company should consider an international venture. What factors make doing business abroad worthwhile? And when does a company have insufficient reason to proceed overseas?

THE WRONG REASONS FOR GOING INTERNATIONAL

Going international can have many benefits, but far too many companies make this potentially good move for bad—or, more often, insufficient—reasons. Many executives misunderstand the real promise of international ventures. Instead of analyzing the advantages and disadvantages of specific options in carefully chosen markets, they press ahead impulsively, often basing their reasons on misconceptions about doing business overseas. The result is often disappointment, or even financial disaster.

Four commonly held but wrong or insufficient reasons for undertaking international ventures are the following:

- To manufacture or assemble goods under tax-free conditions
- To take advantage of cheap labor
- To serve a previously existing clientele
- To acquire an attractive, tax-deductible corporate vacation spot

Let's look at why—in the absence of other, sounder reasons—these are faulty or insufficient grounds for going international.

Wrong Reason 1: Tax-Free Status

To attract foreign investment, many nations offer a "tax holiday" to certain companies, most often those that are either capital- or labor-intensive. A tax holiday generally lasts from five to twenty-five years. Tax holidays tend to increase in length the farther a company moves from urban centers that have adequate infrastructure and skilled labor. So far so good.

The problem is that tax-free status often blinds American business people to all other considerations. Executives look at their profit-and-loss statement at headquarters; they cringe at the sight of what U.S. taxes take out of their bottom line; they fall for the easy temptation of tax-free status overseas. "If we didn't have to pay taxes," they rejoice, "just think of our profits!"

Unfortunately, most people forget the drawbacks.

- *The farther from an overseas urban center (and hence from adequate infrastructure and skilled labor) a company establishes itself, the harder it is to do business.* In remote areas of many countries, electrical power fails frequently; telephone communications are sporadic; bad weather can delay delivery of raw materials, and shipping costs can be exorbitant.

- *The time the company takes to fill an order can increase significantly as a consequence of manufacturing problems and unreliable transportation.* For many of the reasons just listed, delays and expense in acquiring raw materials and shipping finished products may exceed your wildest nightmares.

- *Finding even unskilled labor can prove difficult.* The more remote the location, the less likely it is that local workers will have had any experience—or will even have interest—in working in a factory environment.

- *All overseas ventures—even when tax-free—necessitate additional accounting and reporting procedures.* The cost of accountancy and legal advice may ultimately exceed the value of an enterprise if tax-free status is the only benefit.

Because of these drawbacks, many companies that move overseas never benefit from their tax-free status. The tax-free status itself is not the problem. Tax-free status is, however, small consolation when a company finds itself losing money in a remote part of the world.

Some executives attempt to circumvent the risky aspects of this situation by limiting their venture to assembly operations overseas. They transfer finished components at a low transfer price to an overseas location, thus showing a loss in the United States and avoiding U.S. taxes; then they assemble the products and transfer them back at an unreasonably high transfer price, once again showing no profit in the United States. This method allows the foreign operations to show maximum profits that are tax-free. However, the arrangement violates IRS regulations and frequently results in a net loss anyway.

If your reason for going international is chiefly to reap tax benefits, you should consider seeking a similar advantage in the United States. Many areas of the country offer tax incentives. By taking advantage of them here, you will enjoy a similar benefit without such a high degree of risk. Moreover, both acquiring raw materials and shipping finished products will cost you less.

Wrong Reason 2: Cheap Labor

With certain exceptions (such as Korea and Hong Kong), you should carefully and skeptically investigate countries notable for cheap labor. A production worker who costs twelve dollars per hour in the United States may cost only one dollar per hour elsewhere in the world. However, one well-trained, experienced American worker may produce more than several workers overseas. In addition, some countries have government regulations that virtually require management to hire a large number of workers to do the job that one worker could have handled in the United States. In China, for example, the government used to provide a foreign company with a factory and a full team of employees. The output of that factory, however, may resemble what you could have attained with a smaller staff of American workers. Other countries, such as Singapore, dictate benefits and wages, thus raising personnel costs.

Productivity statistics that are tempting are also often deceptive. Government ministry figures are especially suspect. Even those supplied by international companies deserve close scrutiny. How have these agencies and companies acquired their data? What are their sources of information? Few (if any) companies publishing such statistics run operations either for manufacturing or for assembly in the countries under study. Often their reports are derived from government surveys. The result, unfortunately, tends to be data with little or no foundation in reality.

Wrong Reason 3: Serving Existing Clientele

Some American businesses unexpectedly begin to acquire clients in a particular country or region. These clients may come about as a consequence of foreign business people visiting the United States, or from advertisements in trade publications that have caught someone's attention overseas. In other instances, a U.S. customer establishes operations overseas and turns to his American supplier to continue meeting his needs. One way or another, these unexpected foreign orders provide a pleasant surprise. A potentially dangerous result, however, is that management may conclude that a market exists for their products overseas when in fact no such distinct market exists.

This situation often leads to sloppy thinking—and, worse yet, to sloppy decision making. The illusion of an easy initial success can tempt management to proceed as if every subsequent choice will be successful as well.

Wrong Reason 4: Acquiring a Vacation Spot

Case Study

One CEO visited North Africa and fell in love with Morocco. Imagining frequent trips to this desert kingdom, he established a Marrakesh subsidiary for his firm, which manufactures kitchen cabinets. Unfortunately, he neglected to notice that most Moroccans don't have indoor kitchens, much less kitchen cabinets. The branch operation was a total fiasco. The lure of exotic climes had distorted this executive's previously sound business judgment.

As unlikely as it sounds, some companies undertake international ventures chiefly to acquire a tax-deductible corporate vacation spot. The usual sequence of events is that someone from top management visits a foreign country on business and, finding the locale attractive, inexpensive, and relaxing, suggests to fellow executives that they start a small operation there. "The beaches are nice," he tells them, "and—who knows?—we might even turn a profit some day." His colleagues make their own visits and concur. The company opens a facility that, if nothing else, provides the excuse for tax-deductible junkets. Unfortunately, the ill-planned enterprise flops after a year, costing the firm several million dollars.

Absurd? Of course. But all too common.

To summarize: International ventures often prove worthwhile, but companies sometimes undertake them for the wrong reasons. Tax-free status, cheap labor, preexisting clientele, and suitability as a vacation spot are insufficient justification for going international in the absence of other, better reasons.

However, good reasons *do* exist.

THE RIGHT REASONS FOR GOING INTERNATIONAL

Five sound reasons justify undertaking an international venture. These reasons are the following:

1. Your company is approaching maturity in the United States, and you have the strength and resources to go overseas.
2. Your current trade with overseas customers suggests a potential market and a competitive edge.
3. Analysis of your competitors' activities abroad indicates a potential market, or their activities in the domestic arena indicate that you should go overseas to compete effectively.
4. Demand for your product in the United States is exceptional, and you believe you have a unique product with universal appeal.
5. Demand for look-alike products is high, or your product is sufficiently superior to the competition that it would have international appeal (or would tend to generate look-alikes).

Right Reason 1: Company Maturity

Entering the international marketplace requires time, money, and resources. Unless you have a good track record at home and a history of stable performance, an overseas venture may strain your resources and complicate problems for your domestic operations. You should be sure that your company is meeting the demand for its products and services in the domestic market before branching out into the foreign arena.

Some business people overestimate their company's readiness for going international. A firm that has been in business two or three years may have a record of good growth that tempts management to start looking overseas. But companies in early stages of development rarely have the managerial talent to cope with their growth problems. Such companies have generally not even begun to reach their potential in the U.S. market. Further, companies of this sort often lack the financial resources necessary for start-up operations overseas, for adequate advertising campaigns in an unfamiliar culture, and for extensive marketing. Under these circumstances, underestimating the initial problems of a new international business venture is easy—and dangerous.

If your company has a longer history of good performance, however, and if you have fulfilled your potential in the domestic market, then moving into the global arena may well make sense. Step 1, "Testing the Waters," will explain how to assess your company's prospects and how to select a target market.

Right Reason 2: Current Overseas Trade

Earlier, we discussed how a preexisting clientele in and of itself is generally insufficient reason for going international. If a company's U.S. customers shift some of their operations overseas, doing business with them may give an impression—a false one—of foreign demand for the firm's products. On the other hand, a significant number of orders from one or more countries does warrant further investigation. Orders from customers with no U.S.-based operations suggest a potential market and point to a market niche that closer suppliers are not filling.

If you find yourself in this situation, you should consider visiting your overseas customers to discuss why they are buying your products. Such a visit can be enlightening, and can indicate that you have a sound basis for an international venture. You may find that your customers have not found a competitive product locally; in that

that case, you are at a competitive advantage either because of your product's price or its quality. On the other hand, you may discover that the situation is in fact less promising than you first hoped. You're certainly better off experiencing an early, small disappointment than a larger, more expensive one. In any case, the only way to determine the nature of the situation is to meet with your customers and find out why they buy your products.

Right Reason 3: Market Potential

Doing simple market research or reviewing your competitors' financial statements can give you an idea of the market other firms are servicing abroad. You should look farther than your U.S. competition alone, however. For example, if your business is manufacturing appliances, you should acquire financial and market data on Philips, Telefunken, and other European competitors, as well as on Japanese firms. Similarly, if you are dealing in retail goods, consider visiting at least a few stores overseas. Viewing the products for sale and noting their origins can provide considerable information about the potential in these markets; talking with distributors and potential customers will give you an even more detailed impression.

Another situation that may justify going international is one in which your foreign competitors have invaded your domestic territory. With the global nature of the contemporary marketplace, you cannot count on corporate survival on the basis of U.S. sales alone. Some of your most energetic local competition may be based halfway around the world. If you find that your company is losing sales to overseas rivals, you may have to confront them thousands of miles away simply to retain your home turf.

Step 1, "Testing the Waters," and Step 2, "Learning the Language," analyze these circumstances and suggest ways to proceed.

Right Reason 4: Exceptional Demand for Your Product

Some products catch the whole world's fancy. The companies producing them almost can't go wrong in their marketing plans. American blue jeans are a classic example. From South America to Europe to Asia to the Soviet Union, people love to wear blue jeans. Of course, companies in many countries produce these garments—often violating copyrights and trademark laws—but the authentic item holds a special appeal. A single pair of real Levi's or Lee's jeans sells for hundreds of dollars on the Soviet black market. Similarly, American pop music sells wildly around the world. Even in some of the most anti-American cultures, the same people who protest against the United States simultaneously covet and acquire American-made goods. The upshot of this situation is that some products seem fail-safe overseas.

Assessing *which* products fall into this category is, of course, difficult, and the risks are great. A product with widespread appeal, however, may justify the risk. If the McDonald's Corporation had based a decision about going international solely on reasons 2 and 3 (current trade with overseas customers and analysis of competitors' activities), the company probably never would have taken the Big Mac and Egg McMuffin overseas. Neither reason applied to McDonald's. Before the company's inroads, little or no competition existed in its field. Yet the company's international operations have succeeded literally everywhere. The McDonald's outlet in Moscow, for example, has the highest customer traffic of any in the world. Someone within the McDonald's organization had the foresight to believe that the company's products would have international appeal.

Right Reason 5: Demand for Look-alike Products

Do your products have the sort of appeal that will eventually tempt someone to copy them? Clothing, appliances, luxury food items, and other high-status products often fall into this category. The fact is, if you don't take such products overseas, someone somewhere will copy them and reap the profits. American businesses lose millions of dollars annually to look-alikes and pirated products marketed under their brand names. The businesses that suffer are most often mature companies with established international brand recognition but without appropriate or adequate international operations.

In certain parts of Southeast Asia, for instance, you can buy imitation Rolex and Cartier watches for a small fraction of their cost in the

United States. Similarly, Apple and IBM computer look-alikes have been sold extensively during recent years. Likewise, copies of designer clothes are sold well below the cost of the originals.

Here, as with the kinds of market research already mentioned, you need to proceed in part through "gut feel." However, you can get a sense of the situation by visiting the various countries around the world that might provide customers for your products. Step 1, "Testing the Waters," also suggests ways to analyze potential risks and benefits.

WHY BOTHER?

The preceding discussions of the global marketplace, the complexities facing American businesses, and the wrong and right reasons for going international may have left you wondering why your company should bother in the first place. Isn't the task too difficult? Isn't it too risky?

The answer, as already noted, depends mostly on factors specific to each company. However, the general situation is so significant that you should take special care not to miss the forest for the trees.

- *The U.S. economy is limited in size and growth rate.* Several factors influence the situation. The U.S. population is fairly stable; American consumers' spending power has increased only slowly over the past decade; many products have reached maturity in their domestic life cycle.

- *The world's population is shifting.* Currently, the population of the earth has reached approximately five billion people. By far the greatest growth is occurring in the Southern Hemisphere. By the year 2000, a small minority of human beings will live in Europe and North America.

- *Per capita income is rising in some regions.* Until recently, most countries outside the Northern Hemisphere had only small population segments with any appreciable buying power. Now many nations have become industrialized. Even some previously depressed economies (such as those of India and the People's Republic of China) show signs of remarkable development.

- *Recent changes (like improved infrastructure and communications) are affecting the distribution of goods.* Obtaining raw materials, shipping finished products, and exchanging data are now easier than ever throughout the world and possible for the first time in some areas.

- *Nations have become economically intertwined.* Companies across the world may present as much challenge to American firms as local competitors; there is no commercial safety in geographical distance.

- *Other nations challenge America's economic well-being.* The United States has half willingly, half unwittingly relinquished its economic primacy in the world market. The consequences of ignoring global competition will affect the quality of life in this country for decades to come.

- *Done right, international ventures are fun, challenging, profitable, and rewarding.* The potential benefits—personal and corporate, tangible and intangible—usually outweigh the potential risks.

No single section in a single book can do justice to the size and complexity of the global marketplace today. This overview has served chiefly to sketch the most striking features of international trade and to suggest that many American managers' dreams and nightmares about doing business abroad are equally illusory.

The global marketplace is not a private club that Americans lack the confidence to join. Neither is it a race or competition that Americans can win simply by virtue of being Americans. Like any commercial turf, the global marketplace is both a geographical place—more accurately, a multitude of places—and an intricate web of regulations, financial conditions, supplies, demands, cultural expectations, and ways of doing business. Success in international trade requires nearly the same combination of skills, experience, open-mindedness, timing, and gut-level business intuition that success in domestic trade requires. The specific circumstances you will encounter in the international marketplace differ from those in the domestic sphere. Hence, what you must do to succeed differs as well.

Part 2 of this book spells out the steps necessary to compete effectively as you start doing business abroad.

PART 2

THE ERNST & YOUNG FOUR-STEP APPROACH TO GOING INTERNATIONAL

STEP 1 _____

TESTING THE WATERS

Testing the waters is the process by which your company initially determines its cultural, financial, and organizational readiness for doing business abroad. It is also a process of evaluating the suitability of your company's products for overseas sale, license, or manufacture. In its later stages, testing the waters is a means of identifying the best potential markets to enter and the best methods for succeeding in those markets. In short, this first step is *cursory* research performed on your home turf. It is the international business equivalent of getting your feet wet before plunging into the surf.

Testing the waters is a serious, significant step in the process of going international, and should be approached thoughtfully and executed carefully; because the tasks involved here are relatively theoretical and inexpensive, however, this step is safe even for companies whose executives want only to explore the possibilities of doing business abroad.

GETTING STARTED—COMMITMENT AND PREPARATION

Two conditions must exist before your company undertakes any international venture: commitment and preparation.

Commitment means that you acknowledge the two fundamental aspects of the situation discussed in Part 1:

- The benefits of entering international markets may contribute significantly to the bottom line.
- The task itself—that is, doing business in the global marketplace, involves business practices substantially different from those customary within the United States.

Accepted together, these two aspects of commitment mean that your company is willing to devote *significant* amounts of *time, personnel,* and *money* to master the challenges of doing business abroad. International ventures cannot succeed when undertaken as impulsive, improvised, short-term endeavors. You can't just dabble at going international. On the contrary, commitment to overseas business presupposes patience, tenacity, and strategic imagination.

Preparation is therefore the second necessary aspect of the initial stage of doing business abroad. Preparation means planning the ideal course of action for an international venture, and subsequently following that plan.

If, after reviewing the general reasons for doing business abroad, you believe that your company can achieve both the commitment and the preparation necessary for success in the global marketplace, then you are ready to test the waters.

To guide you through this process, this step explains the following tasks:

- Determining your company's state of readiness
- Acquiring preliminary, basic background information on international trade and various markets
- Establishing possible target markets
- Identifying possible windows of opportunity
- Confirming market readiness by making an "instant gratification" sale
- Acquiring financial assistance for further research
- Developing an initial focus

There is one other consideration, however, before we explore these stages of the process.

For most companies, these seven tasks are best accomplished in sequence. Finishing each task assists in beginning the next. Yet some companies may wish to rearrange the sequence, or even to skip tasks altogether. Perhaps your company is in this category. If so, then you may already have acquired enough background information; you may already know your company's state of readiness; or you may already perceive a window of opportunity. Depending on your company's intentions, structure, and goals, you may therefore end up testing the waters in a somewhat different fashion from that outlined here. If so, fine. This section—like all others in the book—is a compendium of guidelines and suggestions, not an inflexible blueprint to follow line by line. However, *it is crucial that your company accomplish each task in some way at one point or another.*

DETERMINING YOUR COMPANY'S STATE OF READINESS

First, you should make an initial assessment of whether your company is able to benefit from doing business abroad. Whether you should proceed with an international venture is largely a function of whether the firm has sufficient financial, production, and personnel resources to make doing business abroad worthwhile.

An Evaluation Checklist

The following checklist is a simple, preliminary device for assessing readiness. How many of the ten factors listed are present in your situation? Go through the list, indicating yes or no to each factor.

Factor	Present in your situation? Yes	No
1. Interest from company CEO	( )	( )
2. Sales greater than $5 million per year	( )	( )
3. Appropriate growth rate	( )	( )
4. Good capital position	( )	( )
5. Evident foreign competition in U.S.	( )	( )
6. Overseas demand indicated	( )	( )
7. Adequate or excess plant capacity	( )	( )
8. Personnel with overseas sales experience	( )	( )
9. Technological advantage	( )	( )
10. Evident window of opportunity	( )	( )
TOTALS:	___	___

After checking the appropriate response to each factor, total the number of "yes" and "no" answers. Seven out of ten "yes" answers indicates that your company is a prime candidate for going international. More than seven suggests especially great promise overseas; fewer than seven suggests a lower likelihood of success in the global marketplace.

Two caveats, however.

First, this checklist provides only a rough guide for judging the advisability of an international venture. A more accurate assessment requires a more thorough investigation. The rest of this subsection will outline the most critical factors in such an assessment.

Second, the answer to question 1 *must* be affirmative if your company is to have any chance of success overseas. The firm simply cannot succeed in doing business abroad without the commitment of adequate time, money, and managerial resources; and such commitment is impossible if the CEO is negative or indifferent toward the whole endeavor. A "no" answer on this issue essentially dooms the venture from the start.

On the other hand, if the CEO's support is strong, and if six other factors on the checklist look favorable, then you have good reason to proceed with a more detailed evaluation.

Taking the Measure

To determine your company's actual state of readiness, you should consider the following issues:

Present Operational Capability.   First, examine the company's operational methods and attitudes as they relate to the following questions:

- Are company-wide operational procedures able to support an overseas venture?
- Does the firm have sufficient and appropriately trained personnel capable of dealing with international business issues and a variety of cultural expectations? Alternatively, if such personnel are not on board, can the firm afford to hire them?
- Is management sufficiently flexible in its attitudes and methods to adapt to the various requirements of doing business abroad?
- Will the company culture permit the changes necessary for entering the international marketplace?

Current Financial Leverage.   No matter how small, international ventures tend to be expensive. Your company must be prepared to invest heavily in a venture for it to succeed. Consequently, you should consider the following questions and how they apply to your firm:

- Will the company's current financial relationships (for example, with bankers) support this endeavor?

- How much flexibility does the company have in its finances? (A heavily leveraged firm is unlikely to succeed overseas.)
- What sorts of funding can the company acquire?
- Is the firm financially able to carry significant amounts of inventory before sales? To maintain extended payment schedules? To sell on consignment or on letters of credit?
- If necessary, can the company afford to open some form of facility overseas, with appropriate funding for staff and operational costs?

Existing Plant Capacity.   Because of both the risks and the potential rewards of international ventures, initial expansions of plant capacity may be necessary. Ideally, your company should have some degree of excess capacity; otherwise, the firm should be financially strong enough to expand quickly from the outset.

Consider the following questions in light of your own company's situation:

- *At what capacity is your plant currently operating?* The ideal range is about 75 to 80 percent. A higher level of capacity than that suggests a narrower margin of safety if the company were to expand into the global marketplace.
- *If your current excess capacity is small enough that you would have to expand your plant to sell products overseas, is there a specific opportunity that would justify that capital investment?* In some instances, an unusual technological breakthrough or change in currency exchange rates will make the gamble worthwhile. (A later section of Step 1 will discuss windows of opportunity.)
- *What is the proportion of fixed costs to variable costs in producing your company's products?* The higher the proportion of fixed costs, the more advantageous an international venture may become, since increasing your output will result in economies of scale and consequent reductions of per-unit cost.

Present Products and Product Line.   You should examine your company's products—both individually and as a product line—to determine their suitability for overseas sale. Consider the following questions:

- *How appealing will consumers in other countries find your products?* Advice from a consultant with first-hand experience in potential target markets is crucial in this regard.

- *What hidden issues may exist in your products?* Might members of your target markets object to some aspect of your product for religious, aesthetic, or other cultural reasons? Here, too, the impressions of an experienced advisor can be invaluable.

- *Is your whole product line suitable, or perhaps just one or two products?* If the whole line appeals to foreign consumers, so much the better; but even a single product with widespread appeal can justify taking your business overseas.

A useful resource in addressing these issues is the Department of Commerce pilot program called the Comparison Shopping Service. Designed to provide information about markets and products in various countries, this program can assist you in clarifying the suitability of your company's products and product lines for overseas sales. For information, write to Comparison Shopping Service, United States and Foreign Commercial Service (US&FCS), International Trade Administration, Department of Commerce, Washington, DC 20230.

Current Market Penetration.   Finally, you should examine your company's current market share, within both the domestic and international arenas, by asking these questions:

- *What is your current domestic market share?* Will you be able to acquire further points of market share, without excessive cost? Or have you already reached a point of diminishing returns?

- *If your product is already mature within the domestic market, what is its potential overseas?* The product may have tremendous potential in other countries even if sales have flagged in the U.S./Canadian market. For example, the National Cash Register Company reconditions and sells obsolete mechanical cash registers in Third World countries.

- *If you are still growing in the domestic market, will overseas sales help to keep your overall production costs down?*

Reaching a Conclusion to Proceed or Not

How you analyze the answers to these questions will depend, of course, on your company's overall goals and objectives, on its corporate culture, and on its budget. However, a couple of generalizations about the five organizational readiness issues just raised are appropriate.

The following three issues are of paramount importance:

1.   *Operational capability.* Your operational capability *must* be supportive of initial overseas ventures.
2.   *Financial leverage.* Your company *must* have sufficient financial flexibility and leverage.
3.   *Plant capacity.* Your plant *must* have enough excess capacity to handle the new venture or you must be financially capable of expanding rapidly.

The following two issues are less crucial and more flexible:

1.   *Product line.* You may have a product line that is totally acceptable overseas; alternatively, only a single product, or several, may be acceptable, but may be sufficiently promising to justify going abroad.
2.   *Market penetration.* You can take your products overseas at various stages of product maturity. The late stages of the domestic product life cycle may, in fact, be one of the most promising times. On the other hand, your company's continuing growth in the domestic market at a time of concurrent overseas opportunities development can also justify an international venture. Many American software companies, for instance, sell programs overseas whose popularity has peaked in the United States. (An example is Lotus 1-2-3.)

In any case, determining your company's state of readiness brings you to the first in a series of go/no-go decisions. Perhaps your company lacks the financial leverage, the personnel, or the time to undertake an international venture. If so, taking further steps will be unproductive, even counterproductive. On the other hand, your company may possess the resources necessary for doing business abroad. If so, then you should proceed to the next task in testing the waters.

ACQUIRING PRELIMINARY BACKGROUND INFORMATION

Now you should obtain abundant background information about the region or regions under consideration for an international venture, about the characteristic business practices, and about the most promising markets.

This advice may seem to belabor the obvious. How could you enter a market without information about its size, consumer needs, potential advantages, potential risks, and peculiarities? Unfortunately, untold numbers of American business people leap headlong into the global marketplace with scanty, vague, dated, or simply erroneous information. A remarkable number have attempted to start business ventures with no background information at all (see the Case Study on page 44).

From a business standpoint, limited or inaccurate information can be suicidal. Not all Americans overseas end up staring their lack of data so plainly in the face as Sam Parry did, but analogous situations are appallingly common. Ignorance of host-country politics is only one kind of fiasco possible overseas. Ignorance of local tastes, customs, and taboos has also wrought havoc on otherwise well-planned business ventures; representatives of U.S. firms have all too often attempted the equivalent of selling bikinis to Eskimos or ham to Israelis.

What makes these problems all the more unfortunate is that excellent information is readily available from numerous sources. A wide variety of institutions—both public and private—can help you acquire data on countries, markets, or products, and thereby help you explore your options in the global marketplace. Once again, the keys to success are commitment and preparation. You should commit your company to adequate research before making any actual moves, and you should then prepare to use the new information in a systematic, effective way.

Generally speaking, there is no reason to rush the process of going international. Steady, concerted efforts make more sense than a crash program. Thoroughness will serve you better than haste. Accordingly, you should take the time necessary to explore the global

Case Study

Sam Parry was the assistant director of a corporate team investigating the prospects of a manufacturing venture in a small Caribbean country. After six weeks in the field, the team received a request from the government to address the head of state and his cabinet about their proposal. The team spent several days preparing a presentation. At the last minute, however, the project director was called away; she assigned Sam to address the assembled leaders in her place.

Sam had spent enough time helping to prepare the presentation that he felt comfortable with it. He even practiced his introduction to the prime minister—the honorable Mr. Tollis—and to the prime minister's cabinet. Finally, the day arrived for the address. Sam and the team were received at the governmental palace.

Once settled into the prime minister's meeting room, Sam opened the presentation. "Honorable Mr. Tollis," he began, "and esteemed members of the cabinet . . . "

Abruptly, the prime minister interrupted Sam. "Won't you please start over?" he asked with a peeved smile.

Sam was taken aback. He hadn't expected his hosts to be so formal. They always seemed so casual in their open-necked short sleeved shirts while Sam and his team sweated away in their suits. But Sam soon regained his composure. "Most honorable Mr. Tollis and highly esteemed members of the cabinet . . . "

"Be so kind as to begin again," said the prime minister, now visibly annoyed.

"Most esteemed and honorable Mr. Tollis—"

"Perhaps you should start yet again."

Shaken, Sam glanced desperately at his team, then at the government officials surrounding him. The ceiling fans rattled lightly overhead.

One of the cabinet ministers sitting nearby took pity on Sam. Leaning over, the elderly gentleman whispered, "Excuse me, but Mr. Tollis was deposed six months ago. You are now addressing the honorable Mr. Herbert."

marketplace first in a general manner, then in detail, and always with a view to the long term.

General Research

Before taking any other steps, you (or someone within your company) should do some general research. This kind of research is the most basic sort—essentially a process of acquiring information off the shelf. Because the sources are readily available, general research is inexpensive and quick—a good way to survey the world business scene as painlessly as possible.

International Publications.   One particularly cheap, accessible source of information already lies at your fingertips: international business publications. Just as U.S. business magazines and newspapers are invaluable in following developments in the domestic marketplace, so, too, are the international equivalents useful and often crucial in keeping track of changes and opportunities abroad. Such publications can provide, if nothing else, a general background to the business climate throughout the world.

Any American business person even remotely considering an international venture should habitually read the standard publications. The *Asian Wall Street Journal*, the *International Herald Tribune*, *The Economist*, and *International Business* are reliable, up-to-the-minute sources of information on both general and specific business issues worldwide.

Regional Magazines and Newspapers.   Regional and specialty magazines and newspapers will also help you develop a sense of specific markets. Examples are *Euromoney*, *Financial Times*, the *Far Eastern Economic Review*, *Financial Weekly*, and the *Investors Chronicle*. As well as providing data about the conditions and issues characteristic of particular regions, these publications also supply information about your competitors' activities, since many of them carry news about the opening of new facilities.

Incidentally, many of these publications are available through computer databases as well as in libraries. A computer search on particular topics—your company's product, for example, or the state of the economy in certain regions—can provide a detailed portrait for a limited expenditure of time and money.

Government and Corporate Literature

Both public and private organizations can provide extensive information to companies intent on learning more about the global marketplace. Data often include statistics for products or product groups comparable to your own goods or services.

U.S. Department of Commerce.   The U.S. Department of Commerce offers a continually updated database of foreign market research called the Commercial Information Management System (CIMS) to assist U.S. companies in finding and assessing markets abroad. Market data are provided in either report or diskette form for selected products and industries in countries which the DOC feels offer the best opportunities for U.S. goods and services.

For information and prices on this and a wide variety of other Department of Commerce services, write to your local district office or to Export Promotion Services, U.S. Department of Commerce, P.O. Box 14207, Washington, DC 20044; telephone (202) 377-4819.

American Business Conference.   The American Business Conference (ABC) is an organization whose mission is to foster the growth and development of U.S. businesses worldwide. The ABC publishes information about overseas investment, lobbying activities, and member-companies' circumstances in specific countries. In addition, the ABC sponsors informational breakfasts concerning business opportunities in foreign countries. Headquarters for the ABC is located in Washington, DC.

Individual Nations' Embassies and Consulates.   Most countries maintain a trade promotion office in their embassies. To obtain information about current opportunities, policies, or other subjects, contact the trade attaché at the embassy of the particular country under consideration.

Certified Public Accounting Firms.   All major American accounting firms publish informational guides based on data from their foreign affiliates or operations in specific countries or regions. Many accounting firms have been highly successful in providing services to overseas clients; hence, their information about specific foreign markets is often extensive. Information of this sort can help you avoid asking questions or doing research on topics for which abundant data already exist.

Banks.   Commercial and merchant banks compile statistics on overseas trade. Some banks also publish newsletters or brochures about business opportunities in specific countries and regions.

Consultants and Advisors.   In addition to doing your own research, you can obtain information about international trade through consultants and advisors who specialize in providing assistance on this subject. Two options in this regard are:

1.   Hiring someone with international experience to serve as your in-house advisor.
2.   Seeking part-time assistance from an international business consultant.

Despite the expense involved, either of these options will probably save you money in the long run. Some circumstances—such as an early decision to commit your company to export trade or offshore manufacture—may even justify hiring a full-time employee to head your international operations from the start, since an arrangement of this sort will allow you to obtain crucial input during the early stages of investigation and strategic planning.

A sense of hesitation toward the whole endeavor of international trade, however, may just as strongly justify hiring a consultant. The cost will be far lower than the expenses incurred through an ill-considered or badly planned venture; likewise, the money spent on advisory services may ultimately seem insignificant compared to the profits gained through a successfully planned and executed international campaign.

Where can you find these consultants and advisors? You can locate suitable consultants through an executive search firm or headhunting organization; through any of the large international consulting firms; through the major accounting firms; and through other companies with interest and experience in international trade.

ESTABLISHING POSSIBLE TARGET MARKETS

Once you have acquired some initial information, you should use it to establish a list of promising target markets. Specifically, you should analyze your research data using any of several methods, and develop a sense of which countries or regions most closely suit your purposes. Before discussing one of those methods, however, we should note a mistake that's all too common at this stage of the process.

Many American companies attempt too much in their first international ventures. Having previously held off from doing business abroad, their officers now attempt to make up for lost time. But excessive ambition in the global marketplace is as risky as excessive timidity. The initial goal is *not* to take the entire planet by storm. Just as fighting a war on several fronts at once is difficult, if not impossible, going international in more than one region or country at a time is dangerous and unlikely to succeed.

For this reason, you should *narrow the field*. To avoid the risk of doing too much too soon, you should focus on a particular region, country, or area most suitable for your products, services, or overall strengths as a company.

One of the best ways to narrow the field is the "rifle approach" to research. This method resembles the use of a rifle's spotting scopes for target shooting. To shoot accurately, you first locate the target by means of your own vision. Next, you sight the target through a low-power scope. Finally, you zero in on the bull's eye though a high-power scope. This step-by-step process allows greater accuracy than is possible by scanning a wide area with an inappropriately powerful scope at the outset. Translated into business terms, this method proceeds as follows:

1. First, consider a region as a whole.
2. Next, narrow the focus to two or three countries.
3. Finally, zero in on a specific country or market.

Using an Evaluation Matrix

For purposes of narrowing your company's focus in the international marketplace, the evaluation matrix shown in Figure 4 works like a rifle's low- and high-power scopes in target shooting. Using this matrix will allow you to identify goals, eliminate risks, and pinpoint potential opportunities more objectively and efficiently than you would by following hunches and whims alone.

The evaluation matrix works as follows: On the horizontal axis, you list the countries and regions that interest you—for example, China, Southeast Asia, Europe, Latin America, the Caribbean. On the vertical axis, you list the attributes that could affect your decision regarding which regions or countries to investigate. You can specify the attributes in whatever way you deem appropriate, based on your initial research.

You should examine two kinds of attributes:

1. Those relating to the general business, economic, and political climates.
2. Those specific to your industry or product.

You should consider at least the following five fundamental business and political attributes. How you eventually weight them depends on the nature of the activity your company plans within a given region or country.

Political Stability. The stability and durability of a host country's political system obviously affect your long-term potential for profit. The most attractive setting may become the site of a corporate disaster if governmental crises undermine the nation's economic base, or if a new regime takes an overtly anti-business stance. These are the most relevant questions to ask:

- How sympathetic to business is the host-country government?

- How smoothly has power passed from one government administration or regime to the next in recent years?

- What threats (for example, conflict with other nations, class or racial conflict, or insurgency) might endanger the government?

Currency Stability. Similarly, stability of the local currency is important. Two factors are most significant.

First, *how stable is the unit of currency itself?* What is this unit's

FIGURE 4. The foreign market evaluation matrix

ATTRIBUTES	WEIGHTING FACTOR	COUNTRIES OR REGIONS: COUNTRY A	B	C	D	E	ETC.
GENERAL							
1. Political Stability		RS / WS	RS / WS	RS / WS	RS / WS	RS / WS	RS / WS
2. Economic Stability		RS / WS	RS / WS	RS / WS	RS / WS	RS / WS	RS / WS
3. Currency Strength		RS / WS	RS / WS	RS / WS	RS / WS	RS / WS	RS / WS
4. Currency Mobility		RS / WS	RS / WS	RS / WS	RS / WS	RS / WS	RS / WS
5. Tax Incentives		RS / WS	RS / WS	RS / WS	RS / WS	RS / WS	RS / WS
6. Other Incentives		RS / WS	RS / WS	RS / WS	RS / WS	RS / WS	RS / WS
7. Quality of Infrastructure		RS / WS	RS / WS	RS / WS	RS / WS	RS / WS	RS / WS
8. Ability to Serve as Marketing Hub		RS / WS	RS / WS	RS / WS	RS / WS	RS / WS	RS / WS
9. Etc.		RS / WS	RS / WS	RS / WS	RS / WS	RS / WS	RS / WS
COUNTRY / REGION TOTALS (SUM OF WS)							

FIGURE 4. (Continued)

COUNTRIES OR REGIONS

ATTRIBUTES	WEIGHTING FACTOR	COUNTRY A		B		C		D		E		ETC.	
		RS	WS	RS	WS	RS	WS	RS	WS	RS	WS	RS	WS
SPECIFIC													
1. Income per Capita		RS	WS	RS	WS	RS	WS	RS	WS	RS	WS	RS	WS
2. Competition		RS	WS	RS	WS	RS	WS	RS	WS	RS	WS	RS	WS
3. Sales		RS	WS	RS	WS	RS	WS	RS	WS	RS	WS	RS	WS
4. Specific Laws		RS	WS	RS	WS	RS	WS	RS	WS	RS	WS	RS	WS
5. Cost of Labor		RS	WS	RS	WS	RS	WS	RS	WS	RS	WS	RS	WS
6. Labor Productivity		RS	WS	RS	WS	RS	WS	RS	WS	RS	WS	RS	WS
7. Taxes of Expatriates		RS	WS	RS	WS	RS	WS	RS	WS	RS	WS	RS	WS
8. Cost of Raw Materials		RS	WS	RS	WS	RS	WS	RS	WS	RS	WS	RS	WS
9. Shipping Costs, Raw Material, Finished Goods		RS	WS	RS	WS	RS	WS	RS	WS	RS	WS	RS	WS
10. Etc.		RS	WS	RS	WS	RS	WS	RS	WS	RS	WS	RS	WS

COUNTRY / REGION TOTALS (SUM OF WS)

GRAND TOTALS

RS = Raw Score
WS = Weighted Score

recent history? What factors have affected it? What does the currency's forward market indicate about future stability?

Second, *what international currency is the local unit linked to*? The answer to this question is as crucial as the answers to the previous questions, for it determines not just how you price your product on the international market, but also how you maintain your accounts.

Quality of Infrastructure. No matter how stable a country's government and currency are, successful business operations depend on a high-quality infrastructure. In particular, you should examine the nature and quality of the following:

- Factories and other industrial plants
- Access to and quality of ports and port facilities
- Roads and highways
- Rail service
- Local transportation system
- Telecommunications (including telephone, telex, and FAX services)
- International and domestic airline service
- Regional and local airports
- Housing (both for expatriate staff and local labor force)

Laws, Regulations, Taxes. To provide a useful business setting a host country must have a pragmatic set of overall laws, regulations, and taxes. In particular, these must be conducive to a free-market or capitalistic laissez-faire system. Some countries have established laws and regulations so restrictive as to discourage any investment there. Others have less problematic laws and regulations that nonetheless complicate business practices. Given the burdensome consequences of operating in some of these environments, you should investigate all ramifications of legal and tax issues as early as possible. Specific issues to investigate include the following:

- Overall regulations for doing business
- Ownership regulations
- Regulations on expatriates

- Regulations on structure and composition of management
- Taxes
- Tax incentives
- Regulations on transfer of technology
- Patent and copyright issues

Ability to Serve as a Marketing Hub. A secondary but sometimes worthwhile factor to consider is the host country's usefulness as a staging area for business ventures in contiguous regions or countries. Your initial location can allow access to neighboring areas.

From a classic marketing point of view, the procedure is no different from trying to market in the United States. A company starts in one region, then branches out. Entering a particular site overseas is expensive. Rather than establishing a base in each of several countries, your company may do well to consider settling into one of the hub countries—either a financial or manufacturing center or both. These centers generally have regional distribution companies that can help you enter area markets as well.

The hub approach is a highly cost-effective way to spread your business throughout the world. However, the selection of the hub is important. Typical hub choices include the following:

- *Europe:* London, Zurich, Germany, or the Benelux countries
- *Asia:* Singapore and Hong Kong
- *South America:* Buenos Aires, Rio de Janeiro, and São Paulo

Other Facets to Consider. The general facets just listed are the most crucial to consider in a region; they should unquestionably be part of your matrix. In addition, one or more of the following facets may be appropriate to consider if they seem relevant, given your company's or industry's performance and goals:

- Population with a per capita income over a targeted amount
- Existence and strength of competition
- Current gross country purchases of products similar to yours
- Taxes on expatriates
- Labor costs

- Labor productivity
- Cost of raw materials originating locally
- Local participation requirements
- Shipping costs for both raw materials and finished goods

Again, the appropriate list of attributes to consider depends on the factors affecting sales performance and cost of your product.

How to Use the Matrix

Having identified relevant attributes, you can proceed to use the matrix. For each attribute in each country, you should specify a raw score. Rate each item from 1 to 10, with 1 being poor and 10 being excellent. (The rating can be derived from either your basic research or from information that your consultant has supplied.)

You should then weight each attribute according to its significance to your company's product and operations. For each attribute, specify a number from 1 to 10 in the weighting factor column. For example, if your company is considering a major capital investment, then political stability warrants a weighting factor of 10. Similarly, the weighting factor for economic stability will vary in accordance with how much this attribute affects your product. A rating of 10 indicates that the effect is high; a rating of 1 indicates that the effect is minimal.

Once you have finished providing the weighting factors, multiply the weighting factor times the raw score (RS) for each attribute for each country. The result of this multiplication is the weighted score (WS). You should focus on this weighted score for further analysis. Finally, total all weighted scores by country or region to obtain a prioritized list of potential markets. The example matrix shown in Figure 5 indicates that for the product under consideration, Europe is the most desirable market.

You can use this matrix both to assess opportunities and to establish target markets. You should, in fact, use this evaluation matrix as part of an iterative process. That is, you can use it periodically to continue narrowing your list of potential locations for overseas operations. For example, if the initial review indicates that the top priority market for your products is Europe, then you should use the same matrix *employing the same criteria* to identify the specific country within Europe most suitable for operations. Likewise, you could use the matrix to identify a particular city within a particular European nation.

(Note: Once you establish a set of criteria in the matrix, you should not change it—with the exception of additions—as the narrowing-down process continues. Deletions of criteria will skew your results and distort your data.)

IDENTIFYING WINDOWS OF OPPORTUNITY

Completing the preceding tasks will have provided a general sense of your most promising target markets and the most suitable products for those markets. Your data may also have given you a sense of particular niches which your products might fill. Step 3, "Mapping Out a Strategy," will show you how to take your findings and build on them, ultimately developing a strategy suitable for entering a particular market overseas.

Something to consider before proceeding, however, is the prospect of identifying a window of opportunity. A window of opportunity generally results from one of the following:

- A temporary relaxation of one or more constraints normally obstructing vigorous commerce, often a change in currency values or a relaxation of government regulations or obstacles

- A sudden technological breakthrough

- An evolutionary change in customer needs

- An increase in market sophistication

Almost by definition, *windows of opportunity appear suddenly, often without any warning at all.* One of their characteristics is that they tend to last only briefly. To succeed in taking advantage of a window of opportunity, a company must therefore act quickly, exploiting the situation as fully as possible. Hesitant, ill-considered action may mean that the firm loses the chance altogether. And while the risks are high and the venture may seem likely to fail, the potential rewards of exploiting a window of opportunity are often great. (A company culture that is risk-averse, however, may argue against

FIGURE 5. Typical foreign market evaluation matrix results

COUNTRIES OR REGIONS

ATTRIBUTES	WEIGHTING FACTOR	CHINA	SOUTHEAST ASIA	EUROPE	LATIN AMERICA	THE CARIBBEAN	ETC.
GENERAL							
1. Political Stability	8	3 / 24	8 / 64	10 / 80	3 / 24	7 / 56	RS / WS
2. Economic Stability	8	2 / 16	8 / 64	8 / 64	3 / 24	3 / 24	RS / WS
3. Currency Strength	5	1 / 5	7 / 35	8 / 40	3 / 15	5 / 25	RS / WS
4. Currency Mobility	10	0 / 0	10 / 100	7 / 70	2 / 20	10 / 100	RS / WS
5. Tax Incentives	10	5 / 50	8 / 80	5 / 50	7 / 70	7 / 70	RS / WS
6. Other Incentives	2	5 / 10	5 / 10	8 / 16	5 / 10	5 / 10	RS / WS
7. Quality of Infrastructure	9	2 / 18	8 / 72	10 / 90	5 / 45	5 / 45	RS / WS
8. Ability to Serve as Marketing Hub	10	0 / 0	9 / 90	9 / 90	5 / 50	5 / 50	RS / WS
		RS / WS	RS / WS	RS / WS	RS / WS	RS / WS	RS / WS
COUNTRY / REGION TOTALS (SUM OF WS)		123	515	500	258	380	

RS = Raw Score
WS = Weighted Score

FIGURE 5. (Continued)

COUNTRIES OR REGIONS

ATTRIBUTES	WEIGHTING FACTOR	CHINA		SOUTHEAST ASIA		EUROPE		LATIN AMERICA		THE CARIBBEAN		ETC.	
		RS	WS	RS	WS	RS	WS	RS	WS	RS	WS	RS	WS
SPECIFIC													
1. Income per Capita	7	2	14	4	28	9	63	4	28	3	21		
2. Competition	4	1	4	5	20	8	32	6	24	3	12		
3. Sales	8	1	8	5	40	9	72	4	32	2	16		
4. Specific Laws	9	1	9	5	45	9	81	4	36	3	27		
5. Cost of Labor	1	1	1	5	5	8	8	5	5	4	4		
6. Labor Productivity	2	3	6	6	12	8	16	4	8	3	6		
7. Taxes of Expatriates	5	7	35	7	35	9	45	6	30	6	30		
8. Cost of Raw Materials	4	2	8	2	8	8	32	4	16	7	28		
9. Shipping Costs, Raw Material, Finished Goods	3	8	24	8	24	8	24	5	15	8	24		
COUNTRY / REGION TOTALS (SUM OF WS)			109		205		373		194		168		
GRAND TOTALS			232		720		873		452		548		

taking chances with windows of opportunity.) Let's consider each of the four factors that create a window of opportunity.

Relaxation of Constraints

A relaxation of constraints is the type of window of opportunity that is perhaps the most difficult to predict. However, when one occurs, it can provide unusual advantages to a company intent on doing business overseas.

Essentially, what happens is that economic or political constraints of one sort or another suddenly ease, thus creating new opportunities and facilitating more vigorous commerce. The most common event is a change in currency values. Because currency exchange rates have such a pronounced effect on pricing of exported and imported goods, some otherwise promising American products simply end up too expensive to sell well overseas when the U.S. dollar is strong. For similar reasons, foreign products may appeal to American consumers over comparable domestic brands at such times. Yet fluctuations of currency values can provide windows of opportunity to companies able to take advantage of them.

Case Study

A large American manufacturer of processed foods attempted for many years to market its product line in Europe, but the unusually strong U.S. dollar limited the company's chances of attracting European consumers. The Europeans simply maintained their loyalty to local and EC brands.

Then, in mid-1986, the U.S. dollar started to decline in value. Given the new exchange rates, the company's products suddenly became competitive. The firm's international division made a big push to introduce its products—a push that succeeded in establishing the company as a major competitor in the market, and that now appears to have won the company a much larger market share than it had.

Technological Breakthroughs

Technological windows of opportunity are somewhat easier to predict than the economic variety, though they, too, tend to last only temporarily. In a sense, the issue is simple: If your company has developed a new technology, you may have opened a window of opportunity. Entering the marketplace at a time when you are the technological innovator may establish you as the market leader. Technological windows of opportunity do not necessarily involve high technology, though they often do. Some products that seem basic—even homely—can take advantage of windows of opportunity created by a lack of comparable products overseas.

Case Study

In 1976, Digital Equipment Corporation introduced the first minicomputer on the market. DEC initially acquired a 100 percent share of the minicomputer market by default; then other firms developed comparable products. With increasing competition, DEC's market share declined to its current 20 percent. However, DEC remains an acknowledged leader in this technical area and continues to retain its competitive edge.

Case Study

Dale Kirby, a cooper (barrel maker) in Higbee, Missouri, learned in 1985 that executives from the Nikka Whisky Distilling Company of Japan might be interested in purchasing barrels from his shop. After negotiating a contract, Kirby began producing barrels for Nikka. In 1986, production for the Japanese totaled 1,300 barrels and $100,000 in sales. Kirby had found a window of opportunity not because his product was high-tech, but precisely because it was *low*-tech—involving traditional skills of a sort the Japanese found valuable.

In short, taking advantage of technological windows of opportunity does not necessarily require the resources of Bell Laboratories or IBM. All you need is a product or service that no one else previously has been able to provide.

Changing Customer Needs

When legal, cultural, or aesthetic situations change within a particular market, new customer needs can create yet another type of window of opportunity. (See the following Gerber Case Study.)

Increased Market Sophistication

Changing levels of market sophistication provide the final type of window of opportunity. This type of window is more predictable than the others, and a company capable of sensing the new sophistication can, given sufficient technical and marketing creativity, design a response to it.

To conclude: The nature of all windows of opportunity is that they are unpredictable, relatively rare, and potentially risky to exploit. If recognized soon enough and acted upon decisively, however, they can give a company both an initial head start and a long-term competitive advantage.

Case Study

Gerber Products Company has undertaken extensive market research in India. Despite India's predominantly poor population, the country has a prosperous middle class and a small but wealthy upper class that Gerber considers a promising market.

Until recently, most Indians have been unlikely to show any interest in Western-style baby foods. Lately, though, the convenience of such products, plus their status appeal, has heightened consumers' curiosity and openness. Initial focus groups show that baby foods have high potential for success in certain areas of the subcontinent.

Case Study

Sony determined the advantages of and possible customer demand for the compact disc player. After deciding that growing sophistication among audiophiles would justify the expense of developing the necessary technology, Sony created a whole new technology to supplant the cassette player.

In this instance, Sony saw a need for digital audio products, then created the technology to match a higher degree of consumer sophistication. The company created its own window of opportunity.

MAKING AN "INSTANT GRATIFICATION" SALE

Your company has now reached a crucial but potentially rewarding juncture. You have determined the company's state of readiness. You have acquired background information. You have performed sufficient market research. You have identified windows of opportunity. So far so good: You have tested the waters and you like what you find.

Despite all the good information and favorable signs, however, you note with growing concern that everything you have accomplished to date is theoretical. The initial research, the data on company capacity, the preliminary market research, and the other information you have acquired are all on paper. How will your company truly perform in the international marketplace? Perhaps the company will do well, but can you be certain? You would feel more secure if you could simply get a better sense of the situation before committing the company to such a major project.

In fact, you *can* test the situation in a more real way. For this stage in the process of going international is a perfect time to make an "instant gratification" sale—a relatively modest sale capable of demonstrating whether your product *does* appeal to customers overseas, whether it is competitive, and whether the process of doing business abroad will be worthwhile. This kind of sale will also indicate if the product requires any changes. The purpose of an instant gratification sale is not to start full-fledged operations. Rather, the sale serves to test the waters in the most tangible, real-world way. By using one of several short-term means of marketing overseas—a trade mission, brokered deal, or consignment sale—you can discover if the task of doing business abroad truly appeals to you and serves your company's best interests.

A sale of this sort serves five purposes beyond the obvious benefit of profits earned:

1. The sale can pay for part or all of your market research expenses to date.
2. The sale can confirm, refute, or clarify assumptions about the target market based on research thus far.
3. The sale can indicate unexpected windows of opportunity.
4. The sale can provide solid evidence that your product appeals to customers beyond previous market boundaries (or, if its appeal is mixed, the sale can indicate what changes will make it more acceptable).
5. Last but perhaps most important, the sale can give you a sense of satisfaction and accomplishment in actually starting to succeed in the global marketplace.

How do you make this kind of sale? The most common way is through an export trading company. These companies serve as brokers between American manufacturers and overseas distributors. By using an export trading company, you can arrange a test sale of your product without establishing a long-term presence in the target market. The export trading company acquires your stock and sells it at a 5- to 10-percent commission; you then receive payment in U.S. cash. Properly negotiated, the deal allows you to test your competitiveness abroad with minimal risk.

One caveat, however. Export trading companies often insist on exclusive rights extending far beyond the initial arrangement. Such rights may include the right to represent your firm not only in one country, but in all, or the right to represent you long-term. Although export trading companies are often useful, *you should exercise extreme care in negotiations with them*. You should set the shortest possible time limit on the period of representation. If possible, you should make the initial sale a one-shot deal.

For companies that prefer not to deal with export trading companies, another source of instant gratification sales is the trade mis-

Case Study

The United States and Foreign Commercial Service (US&FCS) of the Department of Commerce sponsored a week-long trade show in Paris focusing on American-made apparel. Taking a show of this sort to the fashion capital of the world might seem a hopeless quest; this show, however, had a special emphasis—western attire. The participants brought cowboy boots, hats, and other articles of western-style apparel rarely seen in France outside of movie theaters.

Within three days, all the participants had sold out. One manufacturer ended up selling a year's production in that brief time span.

sion. The U.S. government sponsors and organizes trade missions to foreign countries, thereby providing contacts, publicity, and travel arrangements to participating firms. Although the ultimate success of a particular company's participation depends mostly on its products and marketing expertise, trade missions are a relatively inexpensive means of making initial sales. At times they can prove almost bewilderingly successful.

In short, an instant gratification sale can be bankable proof that your hunches and ideas about going international are as good as you thought they were from the start. Such a sale is one of the best possible ways to test your competitiveness overseas.

FINDING FINANCIAL ASSISTANCE FOR FURTHER RESEARCH

Much to the surprise of most American corporate officers, the U.S. government will help companies conduct research into potential overseas trade. Your company may qualify for a cash grant to investigate international markets and your product's suitability for them.

Once you have developed a list of target countries, you should consider applying for one or more of these grants to fund further research. Several different federal government programs can finance marketing research or a detailed feasibility study. Some of the most promising possibilities include the following:

- *Export Import Bank (Eximbank)*, 811 Vermont Avenue, NW, Washington, DC 20571. Eximbank provides funding to businesses interested in doing business abroad. Programs include the Working Capital Guarantee Program, the Foreign Credit Insurance Association, commercial bank guarantees, and the Small Business Credit Program.

- *Overseas Private Investment Corporation (OPIC)*, 1615 M Street, NW, Suite 400, Washington, DC 20527. In addition to financing insurance programs for investors in foreign projects, OPIC offers specialized insurance and financing services for U.S. service contractors and exporters operating in developing countries.

- *U.S. Department of Commerce, Trade and Development Programs (TDPs)*, Washington, DC 20523. The various Department of Commerce TDPs offer funding for businesses wanting to undertake feasibility studies on international ventures.

- *U.S. Department of Commerce, United States and Foreign Commercial Service (US&FCS)*, P.O. Box 14207, Washington, DC 20044. The US&FCS sponsors trade shows, trade missions, and a variety of informational services on commercial aspects of going international.

Other agencies include the Minority Business Development Agency and the International Division, both part of the U.S. Department of Commerce; the U.S. Department of Agriculture Foreign Agricultural Service; the Small Business Administration; the U.S. Agency for International Development; and the Private Export Funding Corporation. In addition, some state and local governments provide grants for similar kinds of research. (Step 2, "Learning the Language," includes a detailed discussion of federal financial assistance measures; and among them, funds for purposes other than initial research.)

DEVELOPING A FOCUS

Now suppose you have determined your company's readiness; you have conducted sufficient research to see how your product will appeal to certain markets; you have identified several windows of opportunity; and you have made an initial overseas sale. What you should do next is to develop the right focus.

Developing a focus is the process of taking all the information acquired thus far and confirming your goals and objectives as they relate to the prospective international venture. Although corporate officers can accomplish this task through a variety of methods, the most common and systematic way involves reviewing and perhaps adjusting the company's business plan to accommodate an international venture. (A useful resource in this regard is *The Ernst & Young Business Plan Guide* [New York: John Wiley & Sons, 1987].)

To some extent, business plans for international ventures do not differ substantially from their domestic equivalents. The components are similar: identification of a product, identification of a market, plans for a structure (that is, division, subsidiary, and so forth), and development of a budget. Although a formal business plan is ideal, a more informal plan may serve the purpose. Above all else, you should confirm that your company's intentions in the global marketplace complement and support existing domestic goals and objectives. After all, your purpose in going international is not just to start a new endeavor, but to strengthen and augment the firm's activities in the domestic market—in short, to position the company's products better at home as well.

The old maxim holds true here as elsewhere: The best defense is a good offense. Strengthening domestic markets requires expanding into new territory. For example, if a manufacturer of a certain device enters new markets, the increased production for satisfying the new customers' demands will almost certainly reduce the overall per-unit production costs. This will in turn produce two consequences. First, the lower production cost will provide greater flexibility in sales price, thus possibly increasing market share. Second, expansion into new markets presents increased strategic flexibility in implementing tactical market thrusts. The end result will be strengthened company position through increased flexibility for maneuvering in the various markets.

On the other hand, if you determine that your international endeavors will conflict with domestic operations or jeopardize the company's financial stability, then doing business abroad may not be advisable.

This situation leads to the second go/no-go decision in the process of going international.

- *Go*: You have developed a short list of target markets for your products. You now feel even more interested in doing business abroad than you felt before. You want to proceed, narrowing and clarifying your options.
- *No-go*: The result of your initial research is negative. Going international does not appeal to you as much as you first thought.

My experience leads me to believe that executives in most companies have an accurate impression at this stage of whether they should proceed with the four-step process. Generally, the outlook is pretty clear one way or the other.

However, sometimes it's too close to call. If you find yourself in this situation, how can you make a decision? One way is use a checklist similar to the one that started off this section as a means of clarifying the relevant issues one by one.

As with the previous checklist, seven out of ten "yes" answers points to a go decision, while fewer than seven "yes" answers suggests that your decision perhaps should be no-go. But if it's a close

Factor	Present in Your Situation?	
	Yes	No
1. CEO willing to commit to going international	( )	( )
2. Assessment shows good capital position	( )	( )
3. Background research shows demand overseas	( )	( )
4. Matrix indicates worthwhile target markets	( )	( )
5. Window of opportunity is evident	( )	( )
6. Products/product line appear suitable	( )	( )
7. Plant capacity is adequate or excessive	( )	( )
8. Personnel have overseas sales experience	( )	( )
9. Government funding available for research	( )	( )
10. "Instant gratification" sale made	( )	( )
TOTALS:	___	___

call, you might consider weighting your answers. Using the check-list on page 68, answer each question yes or no. Give each "yes" answer and each "no" answer a raw score (RS) of 1. Then put a 0 in the space for the alternate answer to each "yes" or "no." (That is, if your answer to a particular question is yes, put a 1 in the "yes" space and a 0 in the "no" space.) Then allot each question a weighting factor from 1 to 10, with 1 being least significant and 10 being most significant. Multiply the raw score by the weighting factor to produce the weighted score (WS). Add the weighted scores for a grand total. These weighted scores will highlight the strengths and weaknesses in your company's situation as you consider going international.

Note that *you should use this more detailed method of analysis only if the overall outlook is not evident from the simpler checklist.* Don't look around for the trees if you're already standing in the middle of the forest.

Finally, remember that *the CEO's interest in continuing consideration of an international venture is (as before) still paramount.* All the weighted scores in the world won't help you succeed if your company's top officer regards doing business abroad as a waste of time or an excessive risk.

Whether your ultimate decision is go or no-go, you have based it on real data and on a series of analytical steps. Either way, you have decided what is best for your company. If you decide not to proceed, you have reached this conclusion with minimal risk and expense. If, on the other hand, you decide to continue with the process of going international, testing the waters is only a preliminary step. Its function has been to provide an overall cost-effective means to assess your potential success in the global marketplace. Now, provided that your decision is go, you should investigate the situation in more detail and on-site.

And so we turn to the next step in the four-step process.

Factor	Present? Yes (1)	No (1)	× Weighting Factor (1–10)	= Weighted Total Yes vs. No
1. CEO willing to commit to going international	◯	◯	___	___ ___
2. Assessment shows good capital position	◯	◯	___	___ ___
3. Background research shows demand overseas	◯	◯	___	___ ___
4. Matrix indicates worthwhile target markets	◯	◯	___	___ ___
5. Window of opportunity is evident	◯	◯	___	___ ___
6. Products/product line appear suitable	◯	◯	___	___ ___
7. Plant capacity is adequate or excessive	◯	◯	___	___ ___
8. Personnel have overseas sales experience	◯	◯	___	___ ___
9. Government funding available for research	◯	◯	___	___ ___
10. "Instant gratification" sale made	◯	◯	___	___ ___

GRAND TOTALS: ___ vs. ___

STEP 2

LEARNING THE LANGUAGE

American domestic business practices, as noted earlier, often differ from those common in other countries. Attitudes, customs, and expectations about doing business can vary widely from one region of the world to another. Americans who aspire to commercial success overseas should not assume that what makes sense here will always make sense elsewhere; on the contrary, competing effectively in the global marketplace means learning a new language of contemporary international business.

Words are certainly part of this language. Few businesses succeed in the global marketplace without someone in-house able to speak German, Thai, Japanese, or whatever the firm's foreign partners and customers happen to speak. But the issue transcends verbal communication. What we call language includes customer needs and preferences, ways of marketing products, legal issues, and bureaucratic procedures. In short, learning the language of international business involves accepting differences among cultures—in this case, differences that chiefly affect business transactions—and then transforming the differences from obstacles into advantages.

Learning the language does not necessarily mean *agreeing* with another country's way of doing business. Business practices, like other aspects of culture, have developed over the centuries as expressions of local needs, preferences, and ways of life. Many Americans consider foreign business practices strange, overly complex, or counterproductive. But culture is always relative. Business people from other countries have their own misgivings about equivalent procedures and attitudes in the United States. (In both cases we are *not* referring to unethical practices; rather, the issue is what people regard as the "sensible" or "efficient" way of getting things done.) This is the issue: If you intend to profit from the opportunities awaiting you abroad, then you must open your mind to new ideas and new ways of doing things. Business is always an art of compromise.

THE UGLY AMERICAN, INC.

Americans often have been accused of cultural insensitivity. The "Ugly American" is a worldwide stereotype. Unfortunately, the cliché contains more than just a kernel of truth. To make matters doubly unfortunate, American tourists are not the only culprits. American business people also have often been insensitive to many cultures throughout the world.

Too often, American executives and managers speak dismissively and uncomprehendingly of other cultures.

"We'd like to do business in Japan, but the Japanese just don't speak English well enough to make it feasible."

"They paid us ten million lire [or baht, or escudos, or whatever]. Now what's that in *real* money?"

"This country is so inefficient."

"This isn't how we do things back in the U.S."

Immediately following World War II, when the United States was the world's preeminent exporting country, Americans got away with this sort of cultural chauvinism. The reason, however, was not that our overseas customers didn't mind what we said or how we acted; rather, the reason was that only the United States—of all the great industrial nations—had escaped wartime devastation. We Americans possessed the money, the work force, and the natural resources to dominate the marketplace almost regardless of our attitudes. But the situation has changed in the decades since then. The United States now has many competitors. Customers can—and do—pick and choose among available suppliers. The result is that businesses whose executives continue to express the old "Ugly American" attitude are now doomed to failure.

INTERNATIONAL "STREET SMARTS"

Luckily, there is an alternative to the old attitude.

The alternative is to attain a new sophistication in dealing with the global marketplace. To put it another way: The alternative is to get "street smart" on an international level.

International trade uses a specialized language of current conditions and business practices. Unfortunately, many foreign competitors already know this language. The good news is that you, too, can learn the language, and it will serve you well in your effort to do business abroad.

Step 2 provides information designed to help you learn the language of international trade by means of the following tasks:

- Developing an international perspective
- Identifying and overcoming obstacles
- Conducting market research
- Analyzing risks
- Evaluating corporate tax issues
- Exploring available government funding programs and alternative schemes for financing

A brief word before proceeding, however. Some of the issues discussed in Step 2 will resemble those discussed in Step 1. Certain tasks necessary in learning the language overlap with those involved in testing the waters. The reason is that these two steps differ in degree rather than kind. Testing the waters involves preliminary, basic research; learning the language requires more detailed research. Both steps are necessary for most companies, but not for all. Moreover, some firms may wish to delete or modify certain tasks within either or both steps. The specific tasks that you undertake, and the depth in which you pursue them, will depend on your specific corporate circumstances.

For these reasons, some intentional redundancies exist among the preceding discussions and those that follow.

DEVELOPING AN INTERNATIONAL PERSPECTIVE

To put the matter bluntly: Many U.S. business practices are not understood, appreciated, or even tolerated outside this country. American attitudes toward commitment, strategic planning, employer-employee relations, financial and business planning, and even time itself are, generally speaking, not held in high regard outside North America. For this reason, you must develop a background of business knowledge and a repertoire of business skills appropriate to the global marketplace—in short, you must develop an international business perspective.

Elements of this perspective include

- Committing the company to long-term objectives,
- Recognizing the cultural challenges,
- Pledging personnel and capital resources, and
- Developing patience.

Committing the Company to Long-term Objectives

American businesses do not generally focus on long-term planning. During the past thirty years, executives in the United States have tended to stress short-term return on investment, with a consequent emphasis on the quarterly period as *the* unit of planning. Many U.S. companies consider long-term planning to mean planning ahead a year or two—at most, three to five years. European and Asian firms, by contrast, stress a long-term orientation, generally perceived as planning ahead at least ten years. (Grand strategies can extend to fifteen or twenty years or even longer.)

Admittedly, these differences in time sense are partly a matter of opinion. They are a cultural variable. Yet the differences have consequences, and the consequences often work to the disadvantage of American firms.

Case Study

Jake Herbert, the director of a team attempting to sell construction equipment to a Saudi Arabian petroleum company, allotted a year to establish his company as a presence in the region. However, little came of initial efforts. Saudi businessmen often kept Jake waiting; discussions seemed to meander and stray from substantive matters; making even the most basic arrangements took months.

Frustrated, Jake found that he had made little headway even after half the allotted year. Bureaucratic issues were only part of the problem. If anything, the leisurely pace of Saudi negotiations took even more of a toll. Jake eventually concluded that the Saudis had no real interest in reaching a deal. He recommended to his superiors that the company drop Saudi Arabia as a potential market.

Jake ignored two critical aspects of doing business abroad. First, people in other cultures often proceed less directly—and in some cases more slowly—than do Americans. What Jake mistook for Saudi indifference toward his company was in fact the indirect, often cautious pattern of negotiation characteristic throughout the Middle East. Second, people in other cultures use time as a way of testing a potential business partner's intentions. The Arabs, for instance, often want to do business with Americans but distrust our haste and impulsiveness. (Arabs speak with special derision about

American "cowboys"—business people who gallop into town as if in a Western movie, only to rush out again at day's end.) Jake jeopardized his own potential success because he failed to perceive the obstacles that his own impatience created.

The fact remains: If you are tempted to emphasize only the immediate future in your attempts to do business overseas, the outcome will likely be dismal. Foreign competitors will simply outlast you. Their successes will not necessarily indicate that their products are better than yours or that their marketing methods are superior. But their sense of time will give them a critical advantage. Outside the United States, few cultures (if any) view time as we do, as a very scarce, quantifiable substance. Most other cultures have a different sense of time—a sense that nothing is really new, and that anything that claims to be new deserves careful scrutiny and forethought. The result of such differences is plain enough. Unless you are willing to plan farther ahead than a few years, you should probably refrain altogether from international ventures. Your competition, after all, will be busy planning ten, fifteen, or even twenty years down the road.

Recognizing the Cultural Challenges

You should recognize certain other general cultural challenges aside from time sense and deal with them as systematically as possible. One of the most basic challenges of doing business abroad is understanding and respecting the varied ways in which other people live their lives. What makes perfect sense to us strikes others as pointless, silly, or absurd. We in turn often regard foreign customs with bafflement or disdain. We tend to mock, belittle, or ignore what we do not understand. As much as adjusting to another culture offers the potential for insights into human variety and flexibility, cultural differences are nonetheless a common source of friction between people of differing backgrounds. The pressures of business dealings do nothing to make matters simpler.

Four examples:

1. A Chinese may not look you straight in the eye during conversation or negotiation. This is not a sign of weakness, timidity, or fear, but rather of politeness; the Chinese consider eye-to-eye gazing intrusive.

2. A Saudi will take offense if you cross your legs in his presence. Like many other Middle Eastern peoples, the Arabs regard the soles of the feet as unclean; even the sight of them is considered offensive.
3. A Japanese may agree with your statements or answer affirmatively to your questions without meaning to indicate actual approval or intention to follow through. His or her assenting to your words is intended simply to save face for you, and to indicate understanding.
4. An Indian or a Greek shaking his or her head left to right does not mean no, but rather yes.

Understandably, effective interaction with business people overseas requires both respect for cultural differences and specific knowledge of customs in particular regions or countries. General sensitivity is usually a question of attitude. Specific knowledge of customs requires either firsthand experience of the other culture, reliable advice, or training through cross-cultural seminars or other programs. Since culture affects business practices, communication styles, and values, cultural understanding smoothes the path of interpersonal relations and also simplifies the task of making business decisions. The time and money you invest in this regard will pay off in the long run. Shortcuts generally lead straight toward a fiasco.

Besides customs, another challenge involves differences in consumers' tastes and attitudes in other countries. Products currently considered unappealing here may have great appeal overseas. Likewise, products that seem surefire winners in the United States may not appeal to consumers elsewhere. What sells in Peoria may not sell in Hong Kong.

The issue here is not simply the products or services themselves. The challenge of going international also involves adjusting to different styles of marketing. How you package your product is one aspect of the task. Another is how you advertise. Still another is how you deal with distribution networks and competitors. Each case is different, but in all cases you face cultural biases. Accepting the existence of widely varied consumer wants and needs overseas is the first task in surmounting this challenge. The second task is careful market research—a task explored at length later in Step 2.

Case Study

A widely franchised health club opened a facility in Singapore. With its young, urban population and a widespread appreciation of Western culture, Singapore seemed a site destined for success. Moreover, the club's physical appearance and stock of equipment equaled or surpassed that of comparable facilities in the United States.

Yet the club couldn't sign up enough members. Despite the Singaporeans' interest in sports, the club attracted few of them and ended up catering to the relatively small expatriate community instead. Citizens of Singapore felt little enthusiasm for the American-style health club; they were more attracted either to Western competitive sports or to Chinese calisthenics and other traditional Asian forms of exercise.

Case Study

The temporary services company, Manpower, Inc., has adapted to cultural differences in some very creative ways. Manpower has a program for recognizing its outstanding workers in offices around the world. Based on clients' evaluations, star performers are given a distinctive piece of Tiffany-designed sterling silver jewelry. The only place Manpower cannot use this program is in Japan. The Japanese assume that *everyone* is an outstanding performer, and anyone who did not receive an award would lose face and feel compelled to resign.

Manpower's success in the Japanese market, on the other hand, exploits a quirk of Japanese society. Many young women enter the office workforce every year and receive excellent training. If they do not marry after two or three years, however, they lose face and feel they must resign, even if the company would love to keep them. They get a second chance at another company, but again if they are still single after two or three years, they resign. They do not get a third chance. So Manpower has its pick of thousands of well trained, enthusiastic office workers with four

Case Study (Continued)

to six years of experience and can often easily place them with previous employers eager to have them back.

Manpower is also responsive to the marketing instincts and advice of native executives in other countries. The company publishes an external newsletter in several languages for communicating with its clients around the world. The executive of Manpower's Mexican operations asked for the English version of the newsletter to send to his clients. The newsletter goes out to the CEOs of Mexico's biggest companies, who all speak English fluently. The local executive recognized that sending them the English version of the newsletter subtly compliments them on their cosmopolitan skills while emphasizing Manpower's international status.

Pledging Resources

Overseas ventures require a substantial commitment of resources. Few facts about international business are so obvious, yet the challenge of allocating funds alarms many executives. The predictable consequence is that many ventures never get off the ground.

American firms going abroad for the first time tend to underestimate the competence of the local work force. The result is an expensive overuse of American expatriates. You do need personnel from your own country—at least initially—because they know the business, the company, and its preferred ways of operating. However, placing Americans overseas is very expensive. The average foreign posting can cost three times the employee's domestic salary. For obvious reasons, your company should limit the number of expatriate positions to the minimum possible.

With regard to personnel, consider also the following factors:

- The inadvisability of frequent rotation of personnel. Because foreign assignments involve a long learning curve, most expatriate staff members don't reach peak efficiency until their third year. Frequent rotation of personnel may therefore jeopardize a foreign staff's potential in the host country. In contrast to most U.S. companies, European and Asian firms keep executives at their overseas posts at least five or ten years; twenty or twenty-five years is not unusual. Although such long-term assignments may not be realistic for American executives, short postings—a year or two—are often self-defeating.

- *The effects of company culture on expatriate personnel.* Most European companies offer international posts as a sign of faith in an executive's ascent up the corporate ladder. By contrast, American firms—with a few notable exceptions, such as banks and oil companies—sometimes have tended to see the international sector as a pasture for languishing executives. Fortunately, this attitude has begun to change. Attitudes within your company will clearly affect the number and caliber of personnel you can attract for increasingly important assignments overseas.

Ultimately, the issue is whether your company wants the long-term benefits of international trade enough to pledge shorter-term capital resources. Going international is always expensive. Half-hearted, ill-planned efforts will not pay off; in contrast, more thoughtful investments may well yield worthwhile results.

Developing Patience

Case Study

In 1963, Rolls Royce reached an agreement with the People's Republic of China to build a plant for manufacturing aircraft engines. Seventeen years passed without Rolls Royce turning a profit on their plant.

Then during the early 1980s, the Chinese government started ordering large numbers of jets—all without engines—from the Boeing Company. The Chinese wanted the planes without engines because they already have the Rolls Royce engine manufacturing plant in place. Current Chinese plans call for extensive modernization of both civilian and military aircraft fleets, with large numbers of engines necessary for both.

Since 1980, Rolls Royce has turned a profit on its Chinese engine manufacturing division.

Some host countries use tests of patience as a bellwether to determine the degree of foreign companies' real interest. If you are intent on doing business in a particular country, your plans may proceed smoothly and with due speed. On the other hand, you should always be prepared for the long haul.

Your company may not be as big as Rolls Royce, and you probably won't have to wait seventeen years to turn a profit overseas. But the story indicates that certain countries expect a long-term commitment from companies wanting to do business there. Are you willing to make that sort of commitment? Your foreign competitors are almost certainly ready for a long wait. To succeed, you must be ready to make similar concessions. In this respect, as in others, learning the language of international trade is really a matter of developing the competitive perspective.

IDENTIFYING AND OVERCOMING OBSTACLES

The next task in learning the language is to identify and overcome obstacles. Most of these obstacles are artificial, for the most part various sorts of restrictions on free trade.

Many governments give a high priority to developing their local economies and protecting their home markets. Their leaders believe that if a multinational company enters the country, the economy should benefit not just from increased employment, but from other aspects of the operation as well. For these reasons, most countries have established laws that they believe will foster local economic development. Whether they succeed in attaining this goal or not is debatable. In some cases, they do; in other cases, they do more harm than good to all parties concerned. But one way or another, these laws confront virtually any American company intending to go international.

Such laws and regulations vary from country to country. In general, however, there are two kinds: *explicit controls* and *indirect controls*.

Explicit Controls

The most common explicit controls are *tariffs, quantitative restrictions,* and *exchange controls.*

Tariffs.   A tariff is a tax on an imported product. Tariffs serve two purposes: They raise government revenues and they shield a country's industries from foreign competition. With many countries attempting to develop their own industries, tariffs have become an increasingly common means of protecting local products. Malaysia, for example, imposes a 200 percent surcharge on imported cars to protect sales of the Proton Saga, a Malaysian-made auto. Indonesia is developing a semiconductor industry, which it protects through heavy duties on certain electronic chips.

In 1989, the U.S. entered into the international customs classification agreement based on the so-called "harmonized" traiff system. This is an internationally agreed-upon system of classification codes that assigns a six-digit number to every item traded in world markets. Since the same system is used by all countries that have signed the agreement, the system facilitates world trade by transcending language and classification differences between trading partners. For a list of the codes, write to the U.S. Customs Service, 1301 Constitution Avenue, NW, Washington, DC 20229.

Quantitative Restrictions.   A wide variety of nontariff measures also restrict international trade. One of the most common of these measures is quantitative restrictions (QRs). Quantitative restrictions include bans on the import or export of certain products, as well as import/export quotas limiting other products. Although in fact prohibited by the General Agreement on Tariffs and Trade (GATT), certain QRs remain permissible—for instance, those needed to protect local industries from imports that would cause them serious economic damage.

Exchange Controls.   One of the most difficult international business issues is exchange controls. A number of countries restrict or even ban the transfer of company profits to the parent company's nation. Greece, for example, requires government approval for all transfers of funds out of the country; the People's Republic of China prohibits transfers altogether. Other countries have established less drastic but nonetheless restrictive exchange controls. For instance, Brazil allows foreign companies to repatriate a percentage of profits tax-free, then taxes all further profit repatriation at a high rate.

Currency does not become an issue when your company sets up a local operation with intent to use it as a self-financing operation. For one reason or another—perhaps for tax purposes—you may choose not to repatriate the profits at all. The profits show up on the books; at the same time, you maintain a self-sustaining operation inside that country. (A forthcoming section of this step explores issues of corporate tax planning overseas.)

Indirect Controls

In addition to explicit controls, you may have to contend with other, more indirect controls on international trade.

Content Requirements. Even countries that allow relatively unhindered exchange of goods may stipulate that a certain percentage of an exported product must be locally made. Others specify an assembly clause: that is, they require that products not locally made must be locally assembled.

Stipulations for Local Ownership. Some countries require local equity participation in a multinational operation. This requirement provides the government with a measure of control over foreign companies. The specific terms vary from country to country. Requirements may be either explicit or indirect. India, for example, requires that an Indian firm own 51 percent or more of any operations of a multinational company located in India. In contrast, Brazil does not demand local ownership, but the government ties a company's tax rate directly to the percentage of ownership by a Brazilian national. If your Brazilian partner owns only 5 percent of your local operation, the consequent tax rate will be high. If your partner owns 25 percent, the tax rate will be lower. Other countries do not require local ownership at all.

Local participation is not always undesirable. Despite the obvious disadvantages, a local partner can provide advantages as well. A good local partner can provide you with knowledge about the local marketplace, with firsthand expertise about host-country customs and ways of doing business, and with entrées that might take you years to develop otherwise.

Whatever your company's product or service, and wherever you intend to do business abroad, exploring the nature and consequences of these various controls is a necessary first step in learning the language of international trade.

CONDUCTING MARKET RESEARCH

In Step 1, "Testing the Waters," we discussed preliminary research into international markets. Your company should now identify and define foreign markets in more detail. Just as expanding into new domestic territory requires sizing up various factors in the U.S. market, expansion overseas requires thorough, thoughtful market research.

The Need for Objectivity and Expertise

When investigating international markets, most companies should consider seeking assistance from a reputable market research firm or other suitable consultant. This generalization holds true even if the firm maintains its own research department. There are two important reasons for obtaining outside data under these circumstances:

1. In most firms, company culture and politics will distort a study of overseas markets to some extent. This is likely even if top management makes an effort to stay open-minded about eventual decisions.
2. Most companies—no matter how capable—do not have adequate on-site resources for conducting an effective market study in other cultures. Useful market research cannot be done at a distance; it must be done in the field by personnel with first-hand knowledge of that particular market or country.

Ignoring either of these two reasons may result in operational difficulties and loss of revenue at later stages of the international venture, since decisions on how to proceed will have been based on potentially flawed data. Moreover, market research must encompass wider aspects of the targeted countries than those characteristic of domestic research.

Case Study

Mitsui U.S.A., the U.S. arm of one of the big nine Japanese general trading companies, ranks among the top five U.S. exporters with approximately $4–5 billion in U.S. exports annually. As explained by Arthur E. Klauser in a recent speech, the objectives of these trading companies (or *sogo shosha* as they are called in Japan) are "to do business wherever there is business and to stimulate and expand trade flows and create new ones so that more business can be done." Mr. Klauser went on to say that, "*Sogo shosha* are not user or manufacturer oriented, but demand and supply oriented on a global scale."

Japanese trading companies are among the most truly global of all companies, with expertise in all facets of world trade. A demonstration of how these companies use market research in their efforts to introduce new products can be seen in the following example. This example also illustrates the versatility of the *sogo shosha*.

Mitsui U.S.A.'s market research showed potential in the U.S. and European markets for a new type of bottle for shampoo, vinegar, food oil, and other related products. At that time, these products were packaged in glass containers—Mitsui identified a demand for clear plastic bottles.

Mitsui knew of a Japanese chemical company that had developed a product that, when added to polyvinyl chloride resin, could successfully make durable containers.

After surveying the U.S. and European markets, Mitsui U.S.A. arranged for the requisite testing, obtained approval from the U.S. FDA and European officials, and began importing and directly marketing the product in the United States and Europe.

To further enhance sales, Mitsui U.S.A. carried large inventories and worked closely with new customers. Subsequently, the company studied its European operations and determined that savings could be made by establishing a production plant in Europe. With the assistance of the Japanese producer, Mitsui U.S.A. set up a joint venture in Belgium, obtained the raw material for manufacture,

---

Case Study (Continued)

and produced the product for sale in Europe, as well as for export to the United States, until a plant was later established in the United States. ("Japanese General Trading Companies: Their Role and Outlook in International Trade and Development," presented by Arthur E. Klauser at Georgetown University, March 30, 1988.)

Obviously Mitsui's detailed research paid off. Now lets see what happens when a company's research is not thorough enough.

Case Study

Richard Sanderson targeted a prime Asian market for distribution of U.S.-made whiskey. Sanderson's market study indicated that the consumers would be willing to try American brands of liquor for two reasons. First, the taste of American whiskey resembled that of local brands. Second, the characteristically high prices of the local brands would motivate consumers to consider buying American whiskey. Sanderson therefore set up an import company and made arrangements with American whiskey companies to begin exports to this new market.

Within a matter of months, Sanderson had acquired a significant market share. The local consumers did in fact like the taste of the American products. In addition, the American brands sold at a significantly lower price—at least 10 percent less—than domestic whiskeys. Sanderson had successfully challenged the local companies' market dominance.

Eight months after starting operations, Richard Sanderson was arrested by the host country's authorities on immigration violations and was charged by their ministry of commerce with violation of import laws. The American embassy contested the charges, which by all appearances had been trumped up. Eventually, however, the host country closed down the import operation.

In terms of the market itself, Richard Sanderson's assumptions were correct. The host country's consumers liked the taste of American whiskey, and price did indeed provide further motivation. Sanderson therefore had two good reasons for entering the market. However, he failed to explore how his competition would react to his arrival on the scene; he also neglected to assess their influence on the local government. The domestic whiskey producers and distributors were in collusion with host-country government agencies. Sanderson's neglect of these possible factors led to a costly fiasco.

Legal and Regulatory Issues

The second of the two preceding Case Studies underscores an important point. In addition to exploring conventional economic aspects of the target market, you should also consider the legal, regulatory, and political dimensions as well. Specifically, you should investigate the following:

- *U.S. certification and export licensing regulations.* A variety of U.S. government agencies maintain specific regulations on imports and exports. If you fail to supply the necessary information, your company may be subject to fines or criminal penalties. For example, the U.S. government maintains strict guidelines for the export of computer technology. Even some seemingly innocent products must meet the applicable regulations. Export of the toy called Teddy Ruxpin—a talking bear whose speech is generated by a computer chip—involved approval of paperwork similar to that required for export of a small computer.

- *Host-country laws and regulations.* Each country has its own specification requirements, health and safety codes, labor requirements, labor laws, and tax laws. These requirements may or may not prove obstructive to your venture, but you must identify and clarify the issues before proceeding. Malaysia, for instance, held up the marketing of a U.S.-made diet cola for over a year because the country's food and drug administration maintains its own testing standards for synthetic sweeteners.

- *Trade obstacles.* Possible impediments in the form of tariffs, trade restrictions, and certification requirements may complicate your efforts at doing business in certain countries. Some obstacles are of minimal significance, but determining which of them actually affect you will require appropriate attention. For instance, Japan maintains such stringent controls on foreign-grown produce that U.S. firms exporting oranges to that country must deal with more than twenty separate regulations.

- *The nature of the host-country government.* Is the local government responsive in principal to free-market access and competition? If not, you should consider delaying when or modifying how you enter the market, or you should look elsewhere, even if all other factors check out. Unfortunately, some host-country agencies promise more than they ultimately deliver. Even the economic development boards in some countries will mislead potential foreign investors about the terms or conditions likely once a company sets up its operations. To assess the situation accurately, you should interview not only the officials in charge of local economic development, but also American and other foreign business people who have (or used to have) facilities in the area, to obtain the widest possible overview.

Other Commonly Ignored Market Research Issues

The regulatory and legal issues just discussed are too often ignored or given short shrift because they do not fall within the scope of traditional research. Other more traditional aspects of market research also escape the attention of some corporations. These issues deserve at least the attention normally given to standard topics of research within the domestic arena. Your study should explore these aspects of the situation:

- *The possibility of corruption among host-country competition.* What are the ties between companies? Do one or two companies dominate the market? If so, is there evidence of collusion between them? Is there collusion between these companies and the government? Is there evidence of close family ties between government officials and local business people? Even the most promising market can become a trap if local business practices are corrupt or closed to outsiders. Take as much time as necessary to explore local connections.

- *The nature of the local culture.* What are the tastes and preferences of the local populace? Are these consumers likely to appreciate American products? Or will they find them strange and unappealing? One of the biggest mistakes that Americans make is to assume that people in other nations go about their lives much as we do. Consequently, even the most detailed market studies often overlook the fundamental differences of lifestyle elsewhere in the world.

Case Study

The chairman of a large American soft drink company decided that the firm should target Indonesia for sales of its most popular beverage. With a population of nearly 180 million people, Indonesia is the fifth most populous country in the world. Management considered this huge potential market irresistible and worked out a bottling and distribution arrangement to serve the country. The company sold the soft drink syrup to a bottler, who then bottled the drink and distributed it.

Unfortunately, sales were terrible. The drink simply didn't sell. The marketing campaign flopped despite predominantly good initial research, including research into the local competition and government attitudes, because the chairman and his project directors forgot to consider two major factors. First, Indonesia does have 180 million inhabitants, but most of them live in rural areas still functioning within a preindustrial economy. Most Indonesians simply don't have much money. Second, many of them prefer sweet, coconut-based drinks; they are unaccustomed to American-style carbonated beverages. A market for American drinks does exist, but almost exclusively in the major cities. That market—consumers with Western tastes and sufficient disposable income to purchase foreign-style beverages—totals only about eight million people.

In short, basing market projections on raw demographic numbers is a mistake. Moreover, even a potentially appropriate target population may have tastes that an urban American sitting in a corporate office cannot assess.

The most lamentable aspect of these situations is that many companies' field contacts perceive the potential problems and make a point of communicating their perceptions back to headquarters, but top management often overrides the field staff's recommendations in favor of their own biased assessments.

To put the matter bluntly,

- Do not be lulled or lured by numbers;
- Find good market researchers in the field, and let them study local consumers without interference from biased home-office expectations; and
- Above all, listen carefully to what your researchers tell you.

Case Study

EKG Electronics was founded to sell used medical equipment. The company had a unique idea for reprocessing medical equipment and was able to offer its products at prices substantially below those of new equipment. EKG quickly recognized that overseas markets were going to be the lifeblood of the company because domestic competitors (manufacturers of new equipment) were putting up a strong fight with U.S. government regulatory agencies to prohibit sales of used equipment in the United States.

To enhance its ability to sell overseas, the company established a Board of Directors consisting of leading doctors throughout the world. The founder and president of the company traveled to many countries, visiting these and other doctors, and participated in organized trade missions.

The president of the company assured the investors that there would be no obstacles to selling the products. He received strong interest everywhere he went. The primary issue, he encouraged them, was to focus on product reprocessing issues in the United States.

However, when EKG began to offer its products, it became evident that overseas sales were not materializing. In fact, the com-

Case Study (Continued)

pany had not reached a formal agreement with a single overseas distributor.

At this point, investors in the company demanded that EKG obtain professional assistance in international marketing. At the suggestion of an outside consultant and the insistence of investors, the company planned a trip to four priority overseas markets. The trip uncovered some disturbing facts. First, there were government regulatory obstacles to the import of the product. It was found that there might be ways to remove the obstacles, but that it would take months to do so. Second, it was learned that while leading doctors were theoretically interested in using the products, there was a strong resistance from the actual using surgeons and the hospital purchasing agents. Their reluctance was due to the fact that they received payments from the manufacturers when they purchased new products. Finally, difficulties were encountered in two of the countries where potential distributors had been identified. In one case, the so-called distributor had not been in business for many years, but, as he put it, "when the king returns to power, I will be in the best position to sell." According to other businessmen in the country, the king had been deposed 20 years before and expecting him to return was like waiting for the return of the Tsar. In the other country, the distributor seemed legitimate, but there were difficulties in negotiating appropriate margins. Neither the consultant nor the investor who accompanied the president on the trip felt comfortable with this distributor.

As a result of this trip, it became evident that sales were not going to be realized in the near term, and, in fact, might take a few years before reaching significant volume. The investors realized that the few years preceding this trip had been practically wasted from a real sales point of view. The president had visited the overseas markets but did not meet with the right people nor ask the right questions. Consequently, the investors decided not to put any more money into the company and the company went into bankruptcy.

Appropriate Market Research Techniques

Many standard techniques for market research are appropriate in the initial phases of testing the international waters. You can use a variety of research instruments and acquire roughly comparable data. What you should keep foremost in mind is the need to obtain the most accurate, complete picture possible of customer preferences in the target market, and to grasp this picture as fully as possible. As mentioned earlier, you will only get this accurate and complete picture if your research personnel—whether in-house or outside consultants—truly understand the market.

One risk to watch closely is the *effects of cultural bias on research instruments*. U.S. market research firms—regardless of their excellence within the domestic arena—may not fully grasp the subtleties of consumer issues in other countries. Using American-style research questionnaires may prove inappropriate and counterproductive. In some cultures, you cannot ask direct questions of your respondents at all; you must employ a more indirect method instead. (Many Asians, for example, would find direct questioning pushy and offensive.) In other cultures, questions that may seem worthwhile to an American market researcher may prove pointless, awkward, or insulting to respondents. (For instance, interviewing Latin American men about their preferences in household appliances would insult their masculinity, since many of them generally consider the kitchen to be exclusively a woman's domain.)

Respondents may also misperceive some questions that they do answer, thus providing inaccurate data. For example, because Italians dislike the number 7 (it has implications similar to the number 13 in Anglo-American culture), if you use a questionnaire with seven parts or seven questions, Italian respondents may respond hesitantly or not at all. The Chinese, in contrast, believe that the number 8 brings good fortune, so a questionnaire with eight sections may receive a favorable response.

Since few Americans, regardless of their cultural sensitivity, can second-guess all misunderstandings possible in another culture, your team should arrange some sort of *review process* before employing a research instrument in the field. Although such a review extends the duration of learning the language, the expenditure of time and effort is worthwhile. At a minimum, you should have your field contacts try out the questionnaire themselves. A test run among host-country consumers would be a wise investment as well. The same holds true for focus groups or other means of obtaining a first-hand sense of consumer responses (for example, taste testing where applicable). Otherwise you risk skewed data and, in the long run, damage to your whole enterprise.

A Suggested Sequence of Research Steps

If you decide that your company should proceed with independent market research, the process should include the following steps:

1. Defining the market
2. Evaluating market potential
3. Examining market niches
4. Identifying potential regional centers
5. Evaluating present products and product lines

1. Defining the Market. The global marketplace is so complex and competitive that you should strive to be as precise as possible in defining the market you seek overseas. This is especially important if your company is doing business abroad for the first time. You should answer two critical questions in this regard:

1. What is your target market?
2. What is your goal within that market?

For instance, you may have defined market expansion as your goal and Southeast Asia as the target market. Alternatively, your goal may be to introduce a new product, and your target market may be Europe, a market the company already serves. Whatever your choice, you should narrow the market to the greatest degree possible.

Consider your company's product. Where is it likely to appeal most to foreign consumers? Where could it be sold most successfully? How can you test the product's appeal before making more substantial commitments of time and money?

2. Evaluating Market Potential. Equally important are issues of market potential. How large is this market? What is the estimated

Case Study

McDonald's started its first franchise in Japan during the 1960s. Despite the Japanese penchant for fast food, the operation failed to catch on among local consumers for ten years.

Later, McDonald's started conducting extensive market surveys to determine the nature of Japanese tastes. What resulted was a realization that a market for American-style hamburgers did in fact exist, but that the product itself needed to be changed somewhat to accommodate local dietary preferences. The Japanese consumers wanted a sweeter bun, more pickles on the hamburger, and more salt and less fat in the meat. Once McDonald's made these adjustments, their fast food started appealing to the Japanese market. By the mid-1970s McDonald's hamburgers had become a big hit throughout Japan.

Elsewhere, McDonald's has made other adjustments to meet other consumer preferences. In France, for example, the company sells vintage wines as well as popular soft drinks. Customers at McDonald's in Germany can buy local beers. In Malaysia, the choice of milkshakes includes not only the familiar chocolate and vanilla, but also tropical flavors including *durian*—a malodorous fruit popular throughout Southeast Asia.

per capita income of potential consumers? What is the history of consumer demand for similar products? What changes may be necessary in your product before it is appealing?

Another important issue to consider is the deceptive nature of some markets. For example, most American business people would consider India to be a poor market for baby food. The widespread poverty among residents of the subcontinent would surely rule out any possibility of success. Yet the Gerber Products Company has found that the upper 20 percent of India's urban population respond well to test marketing of baby food; the company is therefore operating in India.

3. Examining Market Niches.   Market niches are essentially current and future consumer demands. The demands may be techno-

Case Study

General Electric originally developed the concept of the video cassette recorder, but Japanese electronics firms were the ones who grasped the real potential of the VCR.

The Japanese realized that a whole new market existed among busy professionals who wanted to watch certain programs but couldn't because of business and social engagements. Sony and other firms filled the niche by providing technology to satisfy these customers' needs. People now tape programs while away from home, then watch them when their schedules allow. In short, the concern for flexibility created a market niche that VCRs fill.

logical, aesthetic, or financial; in any case, discovering an unmet demand can provide a niche that other companies have missed.

In dealing with the global marketplace, the most important factor is understanding local attitudes. Some aspect of consumers' needs has not been met, or has not been fully met; this gap provides a potential market niche.

4. Identifying Potential Regional Centers. Another step in market research should concentrate on investigating overseas markets as potential centers for regional operations. If several markets look promising but one of them allows easy access to contiguous countries, then the one capable of serving as a hub for the others is clearly the most promising. Targeting that market now may prevent the later expense of setting up several sites overseas.

5. Evaluating Present Products and Product Lines. Finally, you should return to an issue first raised in Step 1: examining your company's products both individually and as product lines. The initial examination—brief and cursory—met the early needs of testing the waters. Now, however, you should determine specific ways in which your products are suitable or unsuitable.

Consider the following questions:

• Are your products in conformance with tastes, legal requirements, and cultural expectations overseas? Base your answer on previous research—both off-the-shelf and in the field—and, if necessary, on further market studies.

- Are some products suitable while others are not? Is the entire product line suitable? Is the product line perhaps not suitable at all? Here, too, you should perform further sample market testing if necessary.

- If modification is necessary to make a product or the product line suitable, then what are the changes? What level of change does each product require? Have you reviewed all applicable U.S. and host-country laws and regulations? (Some products require such extensive changes that the trouble of making them cannot be justified. For instance, Century Products, Inc., a manufacturer of car seats and other children's gear, found that modifying its seats to meet Sweden's idiosyncratic requirements wasn't worth the trouble. Other products involve virtually no change at all—modification of packaging perhaps. In other cases, you may have to change the products themselves.)

- Are hidden issues present? Might your products offend overseas sensibilities, tastes, beliefs, or preferences, or violate taboos?

By the time you conclude this task, you should have a clear sense of which product or products you intend to take overseas, as well as a sense of which country or region is your prime target market. Are you sure, though? To double-check the decision your company is reaching, proceed to the next task.

ANALYZING RISKS

Throughout this book, I have stressed that doing business abroad involves several iterative processes. That is, you must repeat certain kinds of analysis or planning at different stages of going international. The iterative process just concluded is market research: first the cursory research of testing the waters; now the deeper, more detailed research of learning the language. Similarly, risk analysis—a part of the matrix used earlier—now requires another examination.

Factors to evaluate include the following:

- Political stability
- Currency strength and mobility
- Issues affecting financial operations
- Suitability of the infrastructure
- Capabilities of the work force

Political Stability

Your analysis of potential target markets should consider the various host countries' political stability. In these settings, can there be a successful transition of government without disruption of business? A positive answer does not necessarily presuppose a fully democratic system; some countries have orderly political transition without full-fledged democracy. The most critical factor under these circumstances is whether one leadership or regime can leave the scene and another replace it without resultant political chaos, and without seriously disrupting local business functions. For example, Thailand undergoes frequent military coups, but the political changes have scarcely affected the favorable Thai business climate and the country's steady rate of growth during the past several decades. Other countries, though more democratic in their political processes, have nonetheless ended up with administrations less responsive to multinational companies' needs. (Greece is one such country.)

Currency Strength and Mobility

In Step 1, we touched on issues of currency strength. Now we examine these topics more closely.

The earlier issues were:

- How stable is the unit of currency itself?
- What international currency is the local unit linked to?

Now you should consider how these issues can augment or diminish the risk your company faces overseas.

If your primary balance sheet and pricing strategy is based on U.S. dollars, for example, you will want to enter a country tied primarily to the U.S. currency. Hong Kong, Taiwan, and Singapore all tie their currencies to the U.S. dollar, since the United States is their major trading partner. Fluctuations in the U.S. dollar do not affect the prices of goods bought or sold between the United States and these three Asian countries. On the other hand, if you locate in Singapore but price your goods in yen, fluctuations of the Singapore dollar will make your prices fluctuate as well, causing major accounting headaches.

Note also that certain economic treaties provide stability to otherwise weak currencies. Some U.S. companies are able to operate effectively in European countries with relatively unstable currencies—for example, the Italian lira and the Spanish peso—because the European Currency Unit (the ECU) provides a framework for interchange with the EC. The so-called Snake, to which all EC currencies are tied, also provides some stability.

A final but critical consideration: currency mobility. Many governments restrict the amount of currency that a company can withdraw from the country. You should investigate in detail what percentage of your profits can be repatriated, and under what conditions. The most profitable enterprise in the world will prove pointless if your earnings cannot leave the host country. Greece, for instance, is a potentially profitable market; however, the Greek government limits repatriation of foreign companies' profits.

Issues Affecting Financial Operations

In addition to currency restrictions, other obstacles may affect financial operations. The most significant are the following:

- *Restrictions on local borrowing*. Some countries prohibit multinational companies from borrowing locally. Others require a local partner to take out the loan. Still others require that loans be made in local currency but repaid in a foreign unit of exchange. Determining the nature of such regulations is crucial, since local borrowing may solve some of the currency issues discussed earlier.

- *Restrictions on foreign accounts*. A number of nations restrict the amount of foreign currency that a company can control at any one time.

Suitability of the Infrastructure

You should focus with special care on the host country's infrastructure. The crucial factors are the same as in Step 1, but you should now base your assessment on as much firsthand information as possible, data that either company personnel or hired consultants have provided. The most critical factors remain the following:

- Factories and other industrial plants
- Access to and quality of ports and port facilities
- Roads and highways
- Rail service
- Local transportation system
- Telecommunications (including telephone, telex, and FAX services)
- International and domestic airline service
- Regional and local airports
- Housing (both for expatriate staff and local labor force)

Capabilities of the Work Force

Employment presents two kinds of issues overseas. The first concerns the local work force; the second concerns expatriate staff.

You should consider the following issues that affect the number of available local workers and their quality:

- *Training.* If the local work force in your host country is not trained to the level appropriate for your operations, then you must choose between finding another site or training local workers yourself. Such training programs require additional investment; however, the cost may end up far lower than the cost of bringing in expatriate staff.

- *Unions*. Some countries have more militant unions than others. Depending on the strength and political stance of local unions, an otherwise high-quality work force may prove unreliable.

- *Attitude toward employment*. In the United States, employers and employees tend to see each other in expedient terms. Workers take and quit jobs with varying degrees of commitment; similarly, management hires and fires workers more or less to suit its own needs. Other countries maintain a different attitude toward employment, however. In many cultures, the owners and managers of a business feel a deeper sense of duty toward their employees than Americans expect. The depth of this duty at times resembles that of a parent toward children. The *patrón* in Latin America and the *bapak* in Indonesia are only two expressions of this quasi-paternal relationship. American executives should investigate the local customs regarding their responsibilities toward a host country work force.

As for the issues of hiring expatriate staff, these are so complex that we will address them in a later section. If you feel a need to investigate the question of expatriates now, read the section on this subject in Step 4, "Beating Them at Their Own Game."

EVALUATING CORPORATE TAX ISSUES

Before establishing business operations overseas, you will need to conduct a thorough tax analysis from a global perspective, with a view toward tax reduction and tax deferral. There are many choices: which is the right location, which legal form will be used, and how will the overseas operation be funded; and they all have a tax impact. Also be aware that the U.S. tax code contains many complex rules in this area which can be traps for the unwary. Therefore, it is important to examine the alternatives with the assistance of experienced professional tax counsel who can offer tax planning, as good advice in this area may result in substantial savings.

In evaluating the tax consequences of an overseas operation, you must analyze several basic issues:

- What are the foreign income tax rates that will be imposed on profits generated abroad?

- Will foreign tax credits be available to offset the U.S. tax on foreign income, thereby minimizing potential double taxation?

- Should foreign operations be structured as a branch of the U.S. corporation or as a foreign subsidiary?

- Can tax savings be achieved through intercompany transactions such as loans, licenses, and so forth?

- Can use be made of U.S. tax incentives such as a Foreign Sales Corporation (FSC—pronounced "fisk") or an Interest-Charge Domestic International Sales Corporation (IC-DISC) for exports, or of corporations established in U.S. possessions for overseas manufacturing? (These incentive vehicles are explained below.)

- How will U.S. employees who are sent on foreign assignments be personally taxed?

An overview of the basics of how the United States taxes foreign operations of U.S. companies will help you understand why these questions are important. Briefly, the United States taxes the *worldwide* income of all U.S. persons (including corporations and individuals), except that the earnings of a foreign subsidiary are generally *deferred* until the earnings are paid to the U.S. parent as dividends, or until the subsidiary is sold or liquidated. To alleviate double taxation when income from a foreign source is taxable, the United States allows its taxpayers to credit the associated foreign taxes paid. The overall result of the foreign tax credit rules is that the U.S. corporation eventually will pay the higher of the foreign or the U.S. tax on the foreign-source income. This is important because the 1986 Tax Reform Act significantly reduced the top marginal U.S. tax rates, thereby causing many taxpayers to have excess foreign tax credits. From a tax perspective, you will likely want to minimize foreign taxes without conflicting with other general business objectives. These concepts, with some exceptions, and the planning considerations resulting from them, are discussed in the following sections.

Foreign Country Taxes

Foreign tax liability is often the most important tax issue to consider, and many planning ideas are geared towards reducing it. In evaluating a particular country, first ascertain whether its laws include different tax rates for distributed and undistributed profits, and whether withholding taxes will be imposed upon dividend, interest, and royalty remittances.

Tax Treaties.   U.S. income tax treaty provisions should be reviewed next to determine whether preferential treatment of certain types of income is available. For example, most U.S. income tax treaties provide that a foreign country may not impose its income tax on a U.S. corporation's business profits derived from sources within the foreign country unless the U.S. corporation maintains a "permanent establishment" (e.g., a branch, sales office, factory, warehouse, or other fixed place of business) there. U.S. corporations which derive business income overseas in a tax-treaty country may be able to avoid foreign income taxes altogether where the corporation's fixed facilities are located only within the United States. You have to be careful, though, because locating even an employee or dependent agent* in the foreign country can result in taxable permanent establishment status.

Tax-treaty provisions may also provide for reduced rates of withholding taxes imposed on interest remittances. Many of our treaties reduce the normal foreign withholding rate—often to zero—on interest paid to the U.S. parent corporation. Where this is the case, a U.S. parent might, for example, fund a foreign subsidiary's capital with as much debt as possible, because the interest deductions in the foreign country effectively repatriate earnings at little foreign tax cost. This idea generally works well in high-tax foreign countries. There is a risk, however, that the foreign jurisdiction may treat a portion of the interest payments as nondeductible dividends to the extent the subsidiary's debt to equity ratio is excessive. When that occurs, some foreign countries impose a penalty in addition to the adjusted income and withholding tax. To avoid this, you should determine whether the foreign country provides any "safe harbor" debt/equity ratios and plan to work within them.

---

*A "dependent agent" is an individual who derives substantially all his income from his relationship with a single company. Having a foreign sales representative, for example, whose income consists solely of fees and commissions you pay him—even though he is not your employee and receives no salary nor benefits—can be considered a permanent establishment subject to taxation in the country in question.

Treaties may also provide for reduced rates of withholding taxes on dividends and royalty payments. Depending on treaty provisions and the local tax code, a valid intercompany charge for the subsidiary's use of the parent's patents, trademarks, and know-how can significantly reduce the subsidiary's foreign tax liability and increase the parent's foreign-source income.

If an income tax treaty does not exist between the United States and the foreign country you have selected, one might exist between that country and a third country that does have a treaty with the United States. In this case, you might establish a holding company in the third country through which the dividends or other payments could be made. Caution must be exercised, however, because rules against so-called "treaty shopping" may apply.

Tax Incentives.   Many foreign countries also provide "tax holidays" (i.e., tax reduction schemes) and other local incentives to encourage foreigners to locate operations there. Most of these countries maintain local trade offices in the United States and/or have brochures available which describe the general incentives. Typical tax and non-tax incentives may include:

- A lower rate of tax on earnings to the extent they are retained within the foreign jurisdiction or on earnings from certain favored activities (e.g., high technology)

- Subsidized personnel training programs, or payroll tax reductions for training

- Preferential interest rates on amounts borrowed locally

It should be noted that the incentives can sometimes be negotiated beyond the amounts offered initially, so it often pays to work with independent advisors. It is also wise to get assurances about specific incentives from the local investment authorities *in writing* before committing to a foreign investment.

Foreign Tax Credits

We previously mentioned the United States' worldwide income concept, and that U.S. taxpayers can elect to treat foreign income taxes as a credit against their U.S. tax. A restriction may apply here: The foreign tax credit is limited to the taxpayer's U.S. tax on foreign-source taxable income. To restrict taxpayers in cross-crediting (or "averaging") high-taxed foreign-source income with low-taxed foreign-source income, the Tax Reform Act of 1986 expanded the number of "baskets" into which foreign-source income must be categorized and for which a separate foreign tax credit limitation must be calculated. These include (among others) separate baskets for: passive income, interest income subject to a foreign withholding tax of 5 percent or more, dividends from each 10- to 50-percent-owned foreign corporations, and a general (overall) limitation category. Foreign taxes in excess of the limitation amount for each category may be carried back two years and then forward for five years, but can only be used if sufficient taxable income within the same category is recognized in those other years.

U.S. taxpayers generally strive to classify as much of their income as foreign-source and as much of their deductions as U.S.-source as possible, thereby increasing foreign-source taxable income, which is the basis for computing the limitation.

Corporate Structure

The foreign operations may generally be structured either as a *branch* or as a foreign *subsidiary* of the U.S. corporation. The structure you choose will have a substantial effect on the timing of the U.S. taxation of profits generated abroad.

Branch.   A branch is part of the U.S. corporation and not a separate legal entity; therefore, any profits or losses generated by the branch are currently recognizable for U.S. tax purposes. Where the effective foreign tax rate approximates or exceeds the U.S. tax rate, the foreign tax credit (discussed above) may substantially offset the U.S. tax resulting in little residual U.S. tax liability. In those locations, structuring foreign operations as a branch in a high-taxed foreign country may be advantageous. In addition, an initial U.S. tax advantage may be realized where start-up losses are anticipated from foreign operations. This is because the branch losses would be available to currently offset the U.S. corporation's taxable income from other sources.

The U.S. tax treatment of an interest in a U.S. or foreign partnership (or a foreign entity treated as a partnership for U.S. tax purposes) is similar to that of a foreign branch operation. However, there are several special considerations that may apply and that should be addressed before formation.

Subsidiary. The Uuited States generally defers taxation of the foreign-source earnings of a foreign subsidiary until the income is recognized by the parent company. Where foreign operations are established in low-taxed foreign countries, the use of a foreign subsidiary structure may serve to defer U.S. taxes. This is desirable because the deferred U.S. tax could then be used for expansion of the business or other investments. Subject to anti-abuse rules, this effectively results in an interest-free loan from the U.S. government.

A related consideration is that, when dividends are distributed by the foreign corporation, a deemed-paid, or indirect foreign tax credit is generally made available to the U.S. parent for a proportionate share of the foreign income taxes paid or accrued by the foreign subsidiary. Hence, although the foreign subsidiary may be subject to foreign income taxes on a current basis, payment of the U.S. tax differential (i.e., the U.S. tax liability, less any allowable foreign tax credits) can generally be deferred until the subsidiary's profits are distributed. As a result, planning the proper timing of dividend payments may result in significant U.S. tax savings. Suppose, for example, a U.S. parent needs to generate some foreign source income because it has excess foreign tax credits. As long as the income is within the same limitation category, the parent company could cause a low-taxed foreign subsidiary to pay a dividend, resulting in the "soaking-up" of excess foreign tax credits.

S Corporation. The planning considerations are altered if the U.S. parent company is an S Corporation, and in those cases a foreign branch may be preferable to a subsidiary, because the profits or losses of a foreign branch are "passed through" the S Corporation to its individual shareholders, generally with no U.S. corporate-level tax. Also, foreign income taxes imposed on branch earnings provide the individual S Corporation shareholders with foreign tax credits.

If the foreign operations must be structured as a subsidiary of an S Corporation, note that U.S. tax law requires the subsidiary to be less than 80 percent owned by the S Corporation. Also, while U.S.

tax liability may generally be deferred until the foreign subsidiary distributes dividends, foreign tax credits are available only for any foreign *withholding* taxes imposed on remittances from the foreign subsidiary. That is, deemed-paid foreign tax credits for foreign income taxes paid on the foreign subsidiary's earnings would *not* be available as they normally would be when the parent is a regular U.S. corporation.

Anti-abuse Rules

Deferral of U.S. tax is enticing and many U.S. companies have used their tax-deferred foreign earnings to expand their worldwide operations. Some companies, however, have used the deferral opportunity to invest, in the opinion of the U.S. Congress, in so-called "tax havens" or in other manners contrary to U.S. tax policy. To prevent this, Congress has enacted a number of U.S. tax provisions which may require current U.S. taxation of the subsidiary's earnings (for example, by deeming dividends to have been earned) or have other adverse results. These include: the controlled foreign corporation (CFC), investment in U.S. property, foreign personal holding company (FPHC), and passive foreign investment company (PFIC) rules.

A CFC is a foreign corporation more than 50 percent of whose stock is owned by 10 percent or more U.S. shareholders. The *CFC* rules provide that U.S. shareholders of a CFC are taxable currently on their proportionate share of the CFC's "subpart F" income. "Subpart F" income includes:

- *Passive income.* This category generally includes interest, dividends, rents, royalties, and capital gains from the disposition of assets that produce passive income and which are in excess of certain minimal amounts.

- *Foreign based company sales income.* This category generally includes income derived by a CFC from the sale of goods where (1) the goods sold by the CFC are purchased from, or sold to, a related party; (2) the goods are manufactured outside the CFC's country of incorporation; and (3) the goods are sold for ultimate use outside of the CFC's country of incorporation. The CFC is usually located in a "tax haven" to maximize its advantage. For example, a U.S. corporation establishes a Hong Kong subsidiary which will purchase U.S.-manufactured goods from its U.S. parent for resale by the subsidiary for ultimate use outside Hong Kong. This constitutes foreign based company sales income.

- *Foreign based company services income.* This category is similar to foreign based company sales income and generally includes income derived by a CFC from the performance of services outside of the CFC's country of incorporation where the services are performed for, or on behalf of, a related party. For example, a U.S. corporation establishes a Hong Kong subsidiary to perform engineering services on its behalf outside of Hong Kong. This would be foreign based company services income.

To prevent a U.S. company from directly or indirectly using the earnings of a CFC in its business, Congress enacted the *investment in U.S. property* rules. Investments in U.S. property include (among other things) loans made by a CFC to its U.S. shareholders and third-party loans to U.S. shareholders which are guaranteed by the CFC. Under this rule, a loan made by a CFC to its U.S. shareholders that remains outstanding at the end of its taxable year may be treated for U.S. tax purposes as a deemed dividend from the CFC, resulting in current U.S. taxation.

Also taxed currently is the undistributed *FPHC income* earned by an FPHC. A foreign corporation will be an FPHC where more than 50 percent of its stock is owned by five or fewer U.S. individuals, and where at least 60 percent (normally reduced to 50 percent after the first year) of its income is passive-type income (i.e., interest, dividends, rent, royalties, and so forth). The CFC and FPHC rules require a certain amount of U.S. ownership before they apply. Consequently, it used to be possible to plan around them. To restrict this, Congress enacted the *passive foreign investment company* (PFIC) rules in 1986. A PFIC is a foreign corporation, regardless of U.S. shareholder control, where 75 percent, or more of its income is passive income or 50 percent or more of its assets are passive assets. If a foreign corporation qualifies as a PFIC, an interest charge may be imposed on its U.S. shareholders when they receive a dividend or recognize a gain from disposition of their PFIC stock. Or instead of an interest charge, U.S. shareholders of a PFIC may elect to treat the PFIC's earnings as if they were distributed currently, thereby resulting in current U.S. taxation and the elimination of any deferral.

Many special rules (including complex ownership rules) and certain relief provisions apply to CFCs, FPHCs, and PFICs, necessitating careful planning.

Transfer of Assets

In general, the transfer of appreciated tangible assets by a U.S. taxpayer to a foreign corporation in exchange for its stock will not trigger U.S. tax if the transferred assets will be used by the foreign corporation in the active conduct of a trade or business conducted outside the United States. However, outbound transfers of appreciated inventory, receivables, foreign currency or depreciable U.S. property, among other assets, generally will be taxable.

Intangible assets, such as patents, trademarks, technical data, and so forth, might be transferred to the foreign entity in several ways. These generally include an outright sale (which would cause immediate gain recognition to the U.S. transferrer), a license arrangement, or a contribution to capital. U.S. tax rules restrict the ability of U.S. taxpayers to transfer intangibles as a capital contribution.

Intercompany Transactions

U.S. tax law generally requires that the price charged between related parties (foreign or domestic) for goods or services be the same price that would have been charged between unrelated parties dealing with each other at arm's length. This prevents a U.S. taxpayer from shifting profits to a lower-taxed foreign jurisdiction by means of its intercompany pricing structure. However, the Internal Revenue Service might not object if the intercompany price is *over*stated, resulting in an overstatement of U.S. taxable income. Some companies may entertain this idea, especially now, when U.S. tax rates are low compared to many foreign countries or to utilize excess foreign tax credits. If you are contemplating this, remember that many foreign countries also have arm's length intercompany pricing requirements similar to those of the United States.

In practice, there often is no precise intercompany price that is acceptable for both U.S. and foreign law purposes. The objective is to establish an optimal worldwide pricing strategy by first determining the range of acceptable prices within each jurisdiction. To support the appropriate arm's length price, you may wish to have an economist perform a functional analysis of the activities performed by each member of the related party group. Economic studies are also helpful if the pricing is ever questioned by the U.S. or foreign taxing authorities.

U.S. Tax Incentives

To promote the export of U.S. products, U.S. tax law provides a significant tax incentive to U.S. exporters which establish a foreign sales corporation (FSC) and comply with certain administrative requirements. Thus, U.S. exporters can shift a portion of profits associated with export sales to the FSC, where a portion of it is exempt from U.S. tax, even upon repatriation. In general, FSC tax benefits reduce the federal income tax rate, which is otherwise applicable to export profits, by approximately 4 to 5 percent. Alternatively, an Interest-Charge Domestic International Sales Corporation (IC-DISC) for exporters defers a portion of their annual U.S. taxes on the first $10 million of exports at the cost of an annual interest charge.

There are also tax incentives for certain export activities established and conducted with Puerto Rico and other U.S. possessions.

Expatriate Taxes

Corporations, U.S. citizens, and resident aliens pay U.S. taxes on their worldwide income regardless of their current residence or place of business. Special U.S. tax laws alleviate the burden of double taxation and provide incentives for U.S. individuals working abroad. A U.S. expatriate can elect an exclusion of certain foreign earned income or use foreign tax credits. The foreign tax credit is similar to the corporate rules discussed earlier.

U.S. individuals employed abroad can elect to exclude up to $70,000 of foreign earned income from U.S. taxation if they satisfy certain foreign residency tests. When this exclusion is elected, however, foreign income taxes related to the excluded income cannot be deducted or credited for U.S. tax purposes. This election provides a substantial tax benefit to U.S. expatriates, particularly to those residing in countries with a tax rate lower than the U.S. tax rate.

Despite the benefits of the exclusion and foreign tax credit rules, U.S. individuals working abroad have greater personal expenses and worldwide tax liability than they would have if they remained in the United States. This is because the cost of living may be higher abroad, foreign tax rates exceed the U.S. rates, and duplicate social security-type taxes may be imposed. To encourage U.S. employees to accept overseas assignments, U.S. corporations typically provide expatriate employees with overseas compensation packages which make up for any cost of living differentials and additional tax burdens which are incurred by the overseas assignment. Corporations also provide for children's education expenses, annual vacation, travel back to the United States, emergency medical evacuation, and so forth. As a rough rule of thumb, the cost of maintaining an employee overseas can be expected to be triple his or her U.S. payroll cost, and even higher in places—like Tokyo—where the cost of living is much greater than in the United States.

Compensation packages are additionally expensive because direct reimbursement results in additional taxable income. However, taxes can be minimized with a properly structured package. For example, benefits in kind, such as foreign housing, minimizes taxable income in many foreign countries. Again, before you send an employee abroad, professional tax and employee benefits specialists should be consulted for determining what special planning techniques are available for reducing additional tax and compensation burdens.

LOCATING GOVERNMENT FUNDING PROGRAMS AND ALTERNATIVE FINANCING

The final task of learning the language is a subject introduced briefly earlier: government funding. Like the other iterative aspects of going international, this return to an earlier subject can work to your advantage, since many federal, state, and local government programs provide assistance at this stage of the process.

Specialized Funding for Exports

The U.S. government and many state governments have established programs to assist American companies to export their products and services. Most of these programs—both federal- and state-sponsored—work under the auspices of commercial banks. Consequently, commercial banks are a source of excellent information on available government funding.

The Export-Import Bank of the United States (Eximbank) offers three programs to assist companies with exports:

1. *The Working Capital Guarantee Program* can guarantee working capital loans before actual sales. Although the company takes out the loan with a commercial lender, Eximbank guarantees repayment of 90 percent of the principal, leaving the lender with only a 10 percent risk on the loan.
2. Eximbank's *Commercial Bank Guarantees Program* offers guarantees against nonpayment of foreign purchases on medium-term (181 days to five years) export loans by U.S. companies. Loans can be used for financing capital and quasi-capital goods and services.
3. *Small Business Credit Program.* Since exporters face the risk that their cost of money will rise before a loan is repaid, Eximbank also provides a program to insure small businesses' loans against this eventuality.

For further information on these and other programs, contact the Export Import Bank at 811 Vermont Avenue, NW, Washington, DC 20571. You can also obtain Eximbank publications, including *Eximbank Information Kit*, from the same address. Another useful source of information is the U.S. Department of Commerce publication *A Guide to Financing Exports*, which you can obtain from United States and Foreign Commercial Service (US&FCS) district offices.

Sponsorship and Assistance for Trade Missions

You can undertake trade missions—planned visits to potential buyers or clients overseas—either individually or as part of an organized group. If traveling with a group is preferable, participation in a Department of Commerce-sponsored mission may better serve your purposes. The Department sponsors three types of missions:

1.   *U.S. specialized trade missions.* Department personnel plan, organize, and lead these missions after selecting a product line and an itinerary that offer the best potential for export sales. Commercial officers make hourly individual appointments tailored to the specific needs of each participating firm. Mission members pay their own expenses and share the mission's operating costs.

2.   *State and industry–organized government-approved (S&IOGA) trade missions.* State development agencies, trade associations, chambers of commerce, and other export-oriented groups plan and organize S&IOGA trade missions. The Department of Commerce offers guidance and assistance from planning stages to completion of the mission.

3.   *U.S. seminar missions.* Like trade missions, seminar missions promote the sale of U.S. goods and services abroad; in addition, they assist companies in finding agents and other foreign representatives. These seminar missions are especially appropriate for facilitating the sale of sophisticated products and technology.

Contact the Office of Marketing Programs, Room 2116, Export Promotion Services, US&FCS, U.S. Department of Commerce, Washington, DC 20230, for further information on trade missions.

Other Kinds of Trade Assistance

Several other agencies provide financial assistance to U.S. companies. The most notable are the following:

Small Business Administration.   The Small Business Administration (SBA) established several programs to aid American exporters. Programs include an arrangement with Eximbank permitting certain applicants to borrow up to $1 million through a commercial bank that in turn submits the application to an SBA field office. The

SBA's Export Revolving Line of Credit (ERLC) loan program, meanwhile, permits any number of withdrawals and repayments within the designated dollar limit (certain other conditions apply). Note: To qualify for these programs, a business must meet size and other criteria. For further information on these and other SBA programs, contact the nearest SBA field office, or contact the Small Business Administration, Office of International Trade, 1441 L Street, NW, Washington, DC 20416.

U.S. Department of Agriculture. The U.S. Department of Agriculture, Foreign Agricultural Service (FAS) provides financial support to assist U.S. firms that export agricultural products through the Food for Peace program and the Commodity Credit Corporation. The Food for Peace program authorizes U.S. government financing to companies selling agricultural commodities to friendly countries on concessional credit terms. The Commodity Credit Corporation grants U.S. exporters short-term commercial export financing under the Export Credit Guarantee Program. For further information on these programs, contact the General Sales Manager, Export Credits, Foreign Agricultural Service, 14th Street and Independence Avenue, SW, Washington, DC 20250.

State and Local Program. Almost every state government has an export financing program to assist potential exporters. Some states allow one of their agencies to deliver Eximbank funds, while others offer state-funded loan guarantees.

Investment Protection

Foreign investment in less-developed countries involves a greater financial risk than in other countries. The U.S. government has established an independent, financially self-supporting corporation, the Overseas Private Investment Corporation (OPIC) to facilitate U.S. private investment in less-developed nations. OPIC's purpose is providing investment protection of several kinds:

- Political risk insurance for contractors and exporters, protecting them against the arbitrary and unfair drawing of letters of credit that some countries require;

- Insurance against the risks of currency inconvertibility; confiscation of tangible assets and bank accounts; war, revolution, insurrection, and civil strife; and losses sustained under certain other conditions.

For further information on these programs, contact OPIC at 1615 M Street, NW, Suite 400, Washington, DC 20527.

In addition, Eximbank offers credit insurance through the Foreign Credit Insurance Association (FCIA), which covers 100 percent of a company's losses from political conflict (war, expropriation, currency inconvertibility, and so on) and up to 95 percent of commercial losses (nonpayment due to the buyer's insolvency or default). To learn more about FCIA programs, contact the Foreign Credit Insurance Association at Eximbank.

To summarize, given current U.S. trade deficits, the federal government and most states are increasingly eager to help U.S. companies with their efforts to go international. However, many executives feel hesitant about seeking or using help from the government. The reasons vary, ranging from suspicion of the various agencies' intentions to contempt for their ability to accomplish anything in the "Real World." Such attitudes are unfortunate. Ironically, some of the most skeptical business people are those who simultaneously deride the collaboration between foreign companies and their governments. Why shouldn't American companies similarly benefit from the U.S. government's interest in easing the process of doing business abroad? There's nothing wrong with obtaining well-selected assistance from federal or state governments, especially when it makes a big difference to your company's success, in both the short and the long run.

TO GO OR NOT TO GO?

Having completed all the tasks of learning the language, you have now reached one of the most critical decision points in the course of going international. You have developed an international perspective. You have identified and overcome obstacles. You have conducted market research. You have analyzed risks. You have evaluated corporate tax issues. And you have explored available government funding programs and alternative schemes for financing. Now what?

Unfortunately, this is one of those points when each individual or board faces the decision alone. To go or not to go?

This juncture is an appropriate place for further use of the matrix (Figure 4) described in Step 1. As suggested, the matrix can be modified at each step of going international to narrow the focus of your attention. If you feel some uncertainty about which specific market to enter, for example, you might use the matrix to zero in on particular areas within a country, or even to target individual cities. On the other hand, if you feel misgivings about the regions you've currently selected, you might completely redo the matrix, specifying countries you have previously disregarded.

Overall, the writing on the wall ought to be fairly clear.

If the writing says no-go, then don't. Likewise, if the writing seems a bit fuzzy—or if the words don't seem to have shown up at all—then, generally speaking, the message is also no-go.

If, on the other hand, the writing says go, then it's time to address the issues of strategy and strategic management.

Which brings us to Step 3 in the four-step process.

STEP 3

MAPPING OUT A STRATEGY

For many decades, the U.S. economy grew so quickly and steadily that many competitors could prosper at the same time. More recently, however, several factors—among them the complexity of the domestic marketplace, the scarcity of resources, the expense of money, and the end of constant growth—have changed the rules of the game. The international situation is even more complex:

many nations now compete effectively with the United States. Few organizations can now take survival for granted.

One of the central issues for businesses has become confronting and addressing the challenge of competition. Top management must now focus even more than before on *mapping out a strategy for maximum competitive advantage*. Nowhere is this focus more important than in doing business abroad, where commercial practices and cultural factors are more complex than at home.

STRATEGY: YOUR PLAN FOR COMPETITIVE SUCCESS

Strategy is a plan for action to achieve certain goals within a competitive environment. Whether your goal is winning a football game, increasing market share, or conquering another country, strategy directs the means to the end. A team, a company, or an army might choose to take action without formulating a plan in advance, but even this choice—"winging it"—is a kind of strategy. It's simply an improvisory, spontaneous, confident (perhaps overconfident) strategy. Generally speaking, however, strategy involves conscious, concerted planning. For the most part, strategy requires careful planning focused on the specific goals an organization wants to reach and on overcoming the obstacles between that organization and its goals.

Mapping out a strategy is the logical third step in the four-step process of going international. Testing the waters has given you a general sense of the global marketplace and your company's place within it. Learning the language has provided a more specific impression of how and where your company might succeed overseas. Now the time has come for mapping out a strategy to enter a foreign market. In this step, you can develop a detailed, systematic program for taking your products or services to consumers in another country.

This step—like others in this book—may seem self-evident. What could be more obvious than the need for a strategy in going international? Yet here, too—as with the other steps—a surprising number of companies proceed without well-formulated plans. All too many corporate officers fall prey to the temptation to "wing it." Because other countries seem remote and unfamiliar, it's easy to imagine that improvisation is the only possible way. Many other business people go ahead and develop a strategy but then fail to implement it properly. A third and regrettably common fate befalls overseas ventures when management plans a strategy, begins to implement it, but then loses its nerve or departs unthinkingly from the chosen goals and tactics along the way. The results are predictable: confusion in the field, poor corporate performance, and minimal or nonexistent profits. For these reasons, it is all the more important to plan carefully from the start to ensure successful strategic management.

A note on that last phrase, *strategic management.* In a business context, it's important to distinguish between strategic planning and strategic management. Strategic planning is a method of formulating a strategy that tends to be relatively static. The planners formulate a strategy, then pass it on to the personnel who implement it. By contrast, strategic management is a more dynamic method. Strategic management involves the organization in an ongoing process, and the personnel who formulate the strategy are the same as those who implement it. Strategic management provides a means of integrating organizational capabilities to ensure effective strategic thinking and day-to-day behavior throughout an organization. Strategic management rather than strategic planning is our focus in Step 3.

Careful strategic management is especially critical in the competitive global marketplace. Competitors are abundant; they are experienced and aggressive; they are committed to the long term. Nothing short of thorough, imaginative planning is likely to prevail. However, *the goal is not to devise a strategic plan so extensive that it becomes a burden.* Some corporations have tended to create strategies in such detail—often filling entire volumes—that they serve no practical purpose and ultimately end up ignored and unused. Rather, *the goal is to define the company's mission and how to achieve it, and then to plan a brief, convenient strategy that management will find useful and productive in the course of doing business abroad.*

WHY IS A STRATEGY NECESSARY?

Studies of military history indicate that as a battlefield becomes increasingly complex, strategy becomes more and more crucial. Engaging an enemy in battle and competing against business adversaries have some important similarities. Both require planning. Both involve complex logistics. Both demand imagination, foresight, and steady nerves. Both can result in the loss of territory and resources.

Moreover, both can benefit from the insights of the classical military strategists. Perhaps most significantly—at least for the present discussion—both business and war can involve smaller forces defeating larger, better-equipped ones.

This case study illustrates why a strategy is necessary in going international: to plan for action that will achieve certain specified goals within the highly competitive global marketplace. The Japan-

Case Study

During the late 1960s, Japanese car manufacturers wanted to enter the U.S. market. They looked for a niche and found one at the low end of the market: students and other consumers who wanted no-frills transportation. The small-and-cheap car market, as it so happened, was a niche that did not interest the Detroit auto companies. (Even relatively small American-made cars—such as Ford's Falcon and Fairlane—were essentially family cars.) The only formidable presence in this market was Volkswagen. Even so, VW could not fill the wide-open small-car market fast enough. The Japanese companies responded by following a time-tested military strategy: taking uncontested ground first.

Nissan and Honda first began to introduce their cars into the United States around 1967. U.S. auto makers paid little attention to the newcomers; they derided the Japanese cars as cheap models suitable only for a market that did not interest them in the first place. Essentially, the American auto makers' attitude was to let Volkswagen fight it out with Nissan and Honda. Meanwhile, the Japanese focused on providing low-cost products, built up a following (and, more important still, built up a low-cost, high-quality manufacturing base), then gradually introduced larger, better, higher-priced models.

Now Toyota, Nissan, Honda, Mitsubishi, and all the other major Japanese manufacturers have established themselves as a permanent, formidable presence in the U.S. automobile market. These companies have moved beyond their initial niche to satisfy America's demands for a wide variety of high-quality cars. The Detroit auto makers have had an increasingly difficult time competing effectively against them.

ese auto makers used strategy to take market share from the American companies even though they were competing against unfavorable odds on foreign territory. By defining where their companies had been, where they were, and where they wanted to go, the Japanese developed a plan for systematically achieving not only their ultimate *corporate goals* (taking U.S. market share from the domestic auto makers), but also for achieving the interim *means to the goals* (acquiring an initial niche, then expanding into other niches).

WHAT ISSUES SHOULD A STRATEGY ADDRESS?

While mapping out a strategy, your company should use the information acquired through testing the waters and learning the language to focus on and clarify the following issues:

- Corporate strengths and weaknesses, including products, organizational structure, financial capability, and operational capability
- Corporate goals
- Market trends and opportunities, both current and future
- Market segmentation, including most promising niches
- Competition

In general terms, a strategy should relate the corporation's identity, capabilities, and goals to the nature of the market. More specifically, a strategy provides a means for bringing corporate strengths and weaknesses into the most effective interplay with the competition.

WHAT PERIOD OF TIME SHOULD A STRATEGY COVER?

A good strategy is dynamic; that is, it is flexible enough that management can continually review, evaluate, and change elements of it even in the course of generally successful implementation. As with virtually all other aspects of going international, strategic management is an iterative process. You should not expect to formulate a strategy and then follow it without revision for the indefinite future; you will most likely adjust many aspects of the strategy as you go. Although international ventures invariably require a long-term commitment of time and resources, effective strategic management requires adaptability to future changes, problems, trends, and opportunities.

Generally speaking, no strategy is entirely sound for more than about three years. Circumstances can change drastically over that time span, making predictions risky and the success of recommendations uncertain. Most companies therefore tend to plan three years in advance, while sketching the general contours of later strategy to cover another two or three years. At the year-and-a-half point following initial implementation, management reviews the strategy and adjusts it as needed. Accurate prediction beyond that time horizon is generally difficult, and detailed planning is ineffective or even counterproductive.

There are, however, numerous exceptions to this rule. For instance, the nuclear power industry must plan the construction and operation of power plants to take several decades of work into account. The fashion industry and many high-tech industries such as the computer industry deal with far more unpredictable market demands and far shorter production schedules.

WHO SHOULD PLAN? WHO SHOULD IMPLEMENT?

Given the complexities of strategic management, you must give special attention to the following three conditions if your efforts are to succeed:

1. Management must have a shared vision of the company's ultimate goals. Companies driven by a clear purpose and shared values are far more likely to succeed than those with uncertain purposes and conflicting values.

2. Management must have a common understanding of the company's resources (material, financial, personnel), of its competitive environment (market, competitors, products, critical success factors), and of relevant strategic principles involved.

3. Management must have an across-the-board acceptance of

the direction and urgency of implementing a chosen strategy as the planning process reaches its final stages.

Note that all three of these conditions relate to in-house commitment to the strategy. To put the issue most succinctly, the doers must be the planners. That is, all senior-level personnel should be involved in some or all phases of the strategic management process, and these same people should be responsible for implementing the strategy they decide upon. (The actual degree of their involvement will, of course, depend in part upon the size of the company.)

All too often, top executives keep the planning to themselves and members within the management team. The result is that the people who are most thoroughly involved in implementing a plan have little or no investment in its success. Operations managers can—and often do—simply wash their hands of the strategy if difficulties arise. By contrast, if the persons responsible for implementation are those who helped devise the strategy in the first place, they have bought into the whole scenario more than if they simply inherited a set of advisories from a group of planners.

ONE APPROACH: STRATEGY WORKSHOPS

One successful approach to the early phases of strategic management is to hold in-house strategy workshops. In such workshops, all members of the management team meet to exchange ideas and information; they design a strategy; they plan its implementation. This approach has several important strengths:

- *It promotes the free flow of data* among contributors, thus bringing expertise from a variety of sources within the company.
- *It encourages "devil's advocate" roles* that can increase the chances of spotting potential problems before they occur.
- *It heightens team members' commitment* to the overall plan ultimately agreed upon.

The result of this workshop method is often a high level of participation during planning stages and a greater potential for success during implementation.

Here are three suggestions on how to organize a strategic management workshop:

1. Before holding the workshop, *send each team member a questionnaire* eliciting opinions about the company's strengths and weaknesses, about the competitors' strengths and weaknesses, and about other significant issues to address in the course of strategic management.
2. *Designate one member of the team to facilitate the process.* This should be someone who will encourage new concepts and effective group dynamics rather than foster orthodox company thinking.
3. *Strive for eventual consensus on the strategic plan* rather than forcing an early decision that will alienate team players in the long run. Try to reach agreement on each level of strategy (mission, goals, objectives, and so on, as described in the next section).

The goal of these workshops—in fact, the goal of the planning process itself—is to do the company's strategic thinking as fully as possible in advance. Improvisation has its virtues, and your field staff may have to improvise at times; but the more completely your strategy takes contingencies into account, the more likely your company will be to succeed in its new venture.

A FRAMEWORK FOR STRATEGIC MANAGEMENT

A framework is an essential tool in organizing the tasks of strategic management. One such framework, which we call FOCUS,* has proven effective in a wide range of settings throughout the global marketplace. This framework provides a means for analyzing information, clarifying goals, and planning and implementing corporate strategies. Using this framework can help you create a brief, flexible, practical strategy rather than a long, rigid, overly theoretical strategy of the kind that has burdened many international ventures in the past.

---

*Focus is a proprietary approach to strategic management developed by Ernst & Young and its international affiliates.

What follows is an overview of this framework. You may prefer to use another method—perhaps your company's own in-house procedures—to map out a strategy. But one way or another, you should satisfactorily address the fundamental issues raised in the discussion that follows.

The Three Phases of Developing a Strategy

The FOCUS framework organizes six tasks within three broad phases. These phases and their corresponding tasks are:

- The *foundation phase*, during which you (1) analyze the information compiled from testing the waters and learning the language, (2) define a mission, and (3) establish goals;
- The *strategic development phase*, during which you (4) develop objectives and (5) plan strategies; and
- The *pre-implementation phase*, during which you (6) create action plans.

Figure 6 shows this framework.

The Foundation Phase: Information Analysis, Mission, Goals

In the course of testing the waters and learning the language, you have amassed abundant information about target markets overseas; in addition, you have acquired new or more refined information about your company's operations. Now, during the foundation phase of mapping out a strategy, you analyze this information, with emphasis on the following three areas of concern:

1. Environmental assessment;
2. Competitor assessment; and
3. Corporate assessment.

You then use the results of your analysis to define a mission and establish goals.

FIGURE 6. The FOCUS planning framework

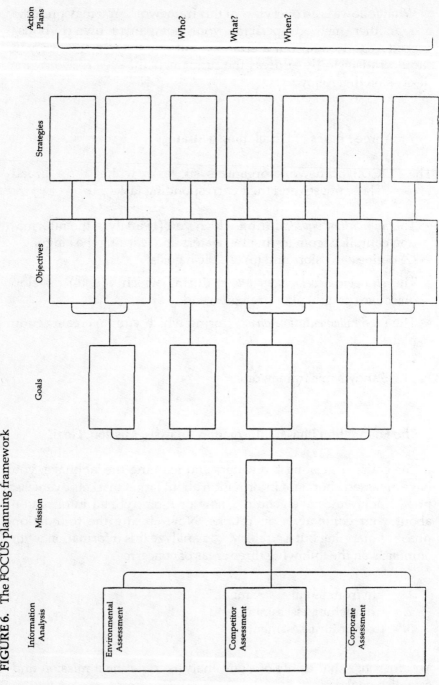

Information Analysis. The task of information analysis begins by assessing the environment in which your company will function overseas. This *environmental assessment* in turn focuses on three subareas: the general environment, the industry, and the market.

First, *the general environment*. What conditions in the host country will affect your venture? Will the climate require special storage facilities for the company's products? How good are the local telecommunications resources? Will host-country financial or political conditions complicate the task of doing business overseas? During the course of testing the waters and learning the language, you have answered these and many similar questions; now you should examine the collected data in terms of how the general environment influ-

General Environmental Analysis

Factor	Asset	Liability	N/A	Explanation
1. Ecological environment (describe):	( )	( )	( )	
2. Technological environment (describe):	( )	( )	( )	
3. Local economic environment (describe):	( )	( )	( )	
4. Demographic and sociopolitical environment (describe):	( )	( )	( )	
5. Legal environment (describe):	( )	( )	( )	

ences your strategy. Use the previous checklist to summarize your data and assess whether each factor is an asset or a liability in relation to your company's plans.

For each factor in the checklist, you should specify the most characteristic features of the target market. For example, a U.S. firm that specializes in alternative energy technology and that is exploring the possibilities of selling solar-powered water heaters in a large Southeast Asian country might specify these features:

1. *Ecological environment.* Tropical climate; two dominant seasons (wet/dry); varied topography (mostly hilly); good maritime access.
2. *Technological environment. Developing technological base; good infrastructure in cities, uneven elsewhere; some hightech industries.*
3. *Local economic environment.* Current economic slump; potential improvement if tin and oil markets improve; governmental constraints.
4. *Demographic and sociopolitical environment.* Growing urban population; large rural population; good work force; ethnic tensions.
5. *Legal environment.* Strict governmental regulations on patent/trademark issues; strong trade barriers; risk of patent/trademark piracy.

The second stage of environmental assessment concentrates on *the industry.* How extensive is your industry worldwide? What corporate structures do other companies use (for example, joint ventures or subsidiaries) in the target market? How do other companies in the industry go about distributing their products? Analyzing these issues will help you identify the factors that influence your strategy for dealing with the industry overall. Use the following checklist in assessing the industry. (As before, you should tailor this checklist to fit the specialized circumstances your company faces overseas.)

The market is the third and final area to consider in an environmental assessment. If a cluster of two countries in a region has high market volume, and if another cluster of ten countries has a lower market volume, which cluster would make the better target market? The answer will vary, of course; but even a huge target

Industry Analysis

Factor	Asset	Liability	N/A	Explanation
1. Industry structure (describe):	( )	( )	( )	
2. Customer base (describe):	( )	( )	( )	
3. Employment and competitive situation (describe):	( )	( )	( )	
4. Business orientation (describe):	( )	( )	( )	
5. Distribution structure (describe):	( )	( )	( )	
6. Safety issues (describe):	( )	( )	( )	

market in terms of area may not be promising if the actual market volume is low. Similarly, the stability of demand influences the decision to enter a specific target market even if the level of demand is currently high. These and other considerations affect your assessment of the target market. Applying your data from testing the waters and learning the language, the following checklist—again, properly adjusted to reflect your specific circumstances—will help you assess the market and its effects on strategy.

Having assessed the general environment, you should now focus on assessing your company's competition. Specific areas to analyze in this competitor assessment are each competitor's market share,

Market Analysis

Factor	Asset	Liability	N/A	Explanation
1. Market volume (describe):	( )	( )	( )	
2. Life cycle status of the market (describe):	( )	( )	( )	
3. Quantitative market growth (describe):	( )	( )	( )	
4. Market share (describe):	( )	( )	( )	
5. Stability of demand (describe):	( )	( )	( )	
6. Market segmentation (describe):	( )	( )	( )	
7. Demand trends (describe):	( )	( )	( )	
8. Structure of customer requirements (describe):	( )	( )	( )	
9. Motivation for purchasing (describe):	( )	( )	( )	
10. Purchasing procedures (describe):	( )	( )	( )	

market segments, recognizable strategies, financial strength, and so forth. Your goal in analyzing these factors is to answer the fundamental questions that will help you plot your strategy. What are your competitors doing? How strong are these companies? What sorts of distribution networks have they established? Why are

Competitor Assessment

Factor	Asset	Liability	N/A	Explanation
1. Market share (describe):	( )	( )	( )	
2. Market segments (describe):	( )	( )	( )	
3. Recognizable strategies (describe):	( )	( )	( )	
4. Present situation (describe):	( )	( )	( )	
5. Price range (describe):	( )	( )	( )	
6. Financial strength (describe):	( )	( )	( )	
7. Reason for current sucess or failure (describe):	( )	( )	( )	

they successful—or why aren't they? Can you outlast them? Sizing up these factors will clarify your strategy in terms of specific rivals. For each competitor, use a copy of the previous checklist (modified in the ways already described) to assess its situation and how serious a threat it presents to your overseas venture.

Finally, the third step in analyzing information is summarizing your own company's situation—the *corporate assessment*. While testing the waters and learning the language, you acquired data about the firm's plant capacity, product suitability, and other factors influencing performance overseas. You should now analyze these areas, with special emphasis on your company's financial resources, knowledge of marketing and distribution, and organizational structure, using the following checklist.

Corporate Assessment

Factor	Asset	Liability	N/A	Explanation
1. Your company's capabilities (describe):	( )	( )	( )	
2. Current market situation (describe):	( )	( )	( )	
3. Research and development capacity (describe):	( )	( )	( )	
4. Production methods (describe):	( )	( )	( )	
5. Procurement methods (describe):	( )	( )	( )	

Corporate Assessment (Continued)

Factor	Asset	Liability	N/A	Explanation
6. Management methods (describe):	( )	( )	( )	
7. Organization and personnel (describe):	( )	( )	( )	
8. Costs (describe):	( )	( )	( )	
9. Earnings (describe):	( )	( )	( )	

One other crucial factor besides those in the preceding checklist deserves your special attention. This factor is your company's *strategic excellence positions*.

Your strategic excellence positions (SEPs) are your company's or product's distinctive capabilities—whatever capabilities make your company unique or remarkable. Properly recognized and cultivated, your SEPs *can give your company leverage to attain success in the marketplace.* For this reason, identifying SEPs lays the foundation for your strategy.

Strategic excellence positions are important because operational excellence alone is not sufficient to guarantee success. Your company's excellence must be in an area of strategic significance; that is, some feature or features of your product or service (or the way in which you deliver it) must be in a position to determine the outcome of competition in the marketplace. For this reason, you should take special care to identify the distinctive capabilities that you wish to emphasize as part of your strategy in going international. Remember in doing so that features that work well at home may not have the same value facing other competitors in other marketplaces.

How do you identify your company's strategic excellence positions? There are a variety of methods, but one of the most straightforward makes use of the checklists already provided in this chapter.

First, go back to the checklists you've used in this chapter. Note all the factors marked on the checklists as strengths. On a separate page, make a list of these strengths. This is your initial compilation of *potential* SEPs. Next, prioritize and clarify the individual strengths. Consider the following questions as you do so:

- Which capabilities of the company are the strongest, the most remarkable, or the most unusual?

- Which capabilities most fully support management's overall goals?

- Which capabilities give the company the most leverage in its new overseas market?

Examples of Strategic Excellence Positions

We can look to a number of corporations for examples of strategic excellence positions. The following companies have achieved success by capitalizing on distinctive capabilities:

3M—product innovation
Chapparal Steel—production technology
Allersuisse—materials technology
Benetton—customer needs
IBM—customer service
Frito-Lay—distribution network
Rolls Royce—image
Disney—employee motivation
GE—strategic planning

As you proceed, you should discard factors that are less promising and retain those that are relatively more so. Narrow the list to three or four strengths. You may wish to regard several of these strengths as your company's SEPs; on the other hand, some firms (like those listed in the preceding boxed example) emphasize one predominant SEP. In any case, you *cannot* have a strategic excellence position that has not appeared initially as one of the strengths in the checklists you filled out.

This process determines your strategic excellence position or positions. In addition, by helping you clarify the issue of the company's strength, it also leads to the next task in the foundation phase.

Mission. After having assessed the environment, the competition, and your own company, and after having identified your SEPs, your next task is to define the company's mission.

In broad conceptual terms, the mission statement defines your company's view of what drives its business activities. The statement may include references to product, target market, desired market position, financial goals, business methods, distribution channels, and geography. Unlike other components of your strategy, the mission statement is not quantifiable or measurable. It may consist of a statement about today's business, or about where the organization would like to be in the future. There are few rules for writing mission statements. A company's mission is, after all, an expression of corporate identity or philosophy, hence something that varies greatly from one organization to another.

Note that an effective mission statement is generally oriented primarily toward your company's customers rather than toward its owners; it does not apply equally well to your company's competi-

Sample Mission Statement

One company formulated the following mission statement: "To be the world leader in developing, manufacturing and selling instruments for laser surgery." We'll call this company Las-Tech, Inc., and use it as a model to illustrate the remaining strategic management tasks.

tors; and it expresses a vision and purpose that employees are proud to work toward.

Goal.   Goals elaborate and expand on key components of the mission statement. Although more specific than the mission statement, goals are nonetheless broad statements of the organization's aspirations for the future. They include the company's distinctive capabilities and, generally speaking, its enduring general features, often nonquantifiable. Most companies state their goals in terms of the external business environment, and often in relative terms— that is, "the leading," "the best," "the highest quality," and so forth.
There are several important aspects of goals:

- Goals can be product-, market-, or function-related.
- The number of goals that a company can achieve is limited, given finite resources. Ideally, a firm should attempt to set only four to six goals.
- Goals must harmonize with each other.
- If possible, goals should build on strengths already present within the organization.

Sample Goal Statements

Las-Tech formulated the following statements:
   Product leadership: To be recognized as having the most innovative and highest-performance products.
   Domestic growth: Expand the use of surgical laser technology until it becomes part of the American surgeon's standard equipment, while maintaining our market share.
   International growth: Establish our firm as the premier supplier of laser surgery technology in the European market.
   Profitability: Earn a return on investment sufficient to attract financial resources to fund our growth and product leadership.

The Strategic Development Phase:
Objectives and Strategies

Objectives and strategies provide the link between the general goals and the specific actions that you will take to accomplish those goals. During the strategic development phase, you create this link.

- *Objectives* quantify the goals.
- *Strategies* make it possible for you to attain these objectives.

Objectives.   Objectives are time-specific, measurable (or at least in some fashion quantifiable) achievements. Obtained from specific departments or people, they are internally focused, indicating desired results in financial or quantifiable terms. Performance against measurable objectives is the prime indicator of whether the company is attaining the related goals.

Sample Objective Statements

Here are the objective statements developed by Las-Tech:
New products: Introduce devices for use in at least three new major branches of surgery within three years.
Existing products: Reduce the user costs of existing devices by 20 percent per year over each of the next five years, while improving performance characteristics.

Domestic growth:

- Have one of our devices installed in 80 percent of U.S. teaching hospitals.
- Expand the use of the technology to at least five new major surgical applications within the next four years.

International market entry: Enter Europe by having one of our devices installed in at least 200 English, French, and German teaching hospitals by 1995.
Profitability: Attain return on equity at above 20 percent.

Strategies. In contrast, strategies describe overall approaches to achieving goals and objectives. They identify the opportunities to be exploited and, in turn, the resources to be acquired and concentrated so that you can take advantage of the opportunities. Strategies are generally sustained over the long term, though they may require fine-tuning along the way. Strategies are not detailed action steps; instead, they define the framework for developing specific action plans and the responsibilities for getting things done.

Sample Strategy Statements

Las-Tech stated its strategies as follows:
New products:

- Double the funding level for our three existing product introduction teams
- Establish three new teams during the next twelve months

Existing products:

- Commit $250,000 to develop a long-term productivity improvement program
- Establish joint research projects with teaching hospitals and major university laser technology departments

Growth:

- Undertake demonstration educational programs covering target markets in the United States and abroad
- Develop innovative financing schemes for initial placements
- Complete substitution of own sales force for agencies by 1990
- Develop and implement a marketing program including advertising, speakers, and technical articles
- Selectively fund high-profile use of our devices

Sample Strategy Statements, (Continued)

European market entry:

- Establish European hub office in London
- Establish branch offices in Frankfurt and Paris
- Hire and train sales force for all three offices
- Establish contacts in major English, French, and German hospitals
- Adapt sales materials to each language/culture, with individual marketing programs including advertising, speakers, and technical articles

Profitability:

- Actively seek external research financing and investigate R&D partnerships
- Raise debt/equity ratio limit to 3:1

The Pre-implementation Phase: Action Plans

We now arrive at the third phase of mapping out a strategy. Backing up each strategy is an action plan and, in turn, an appropriate allocation of resources.

Action plans are essentially the how-to of executing a strategy. They take the form of lists that specify who will do what and by what time. In the case of international ventures, action plans provide the means to track how personnel in the field are executing the instructions that will ultimately set up operations and keep them running.

Sample Action Plan

Here is the action plan Las-Tech formulated to implement one aspect of its goal of international growth.

Goal: Establish our firm as the premier supplier of laser surgery technology in the European market.

Objective: Enter Europe by having one of our devices installed in at least 200 English, French, and German teaching hospitals by 1995.

Strategy: Adapt sales materials to each language/culture, with individual marketing programs including advertising speakers, and technical articles.

Action plan: Develop promotional materials.

Action steps:	Person responsible:	Due date:
Retool promotional brochures to address specific cultural issues within target host countries	C. Girard M. Flannery	May 1, 1991
Identify translation services and request bids for work; select best bidder	R. Levine	May 1, 1991
Submit translated documents to objective third-party medical contact for quality control	M. Flannery	June 8, 1991
Send appropriate materials to established contacts overseas	C. Girard	September 1, 1991

Putting It All Together

The result of finishing the six tasks that comprise the FOCUS framework is typically a document that looks something like Figure 7.

This framework now provides a succinct, easily reviewed map for each officer in your company to follow according to his or her specific role. It also offers a reality check as you proceed to implement the strategy. The FOCUS framework allows easy reference to the chain of cause-and-effect relationships within a particular strategy; that is, the framework's structure facilitates the recurrent task of identifying problems during the course of implementation. A difficulty in executing a particular action plan, for instance, may jeopardize the company's ability to execute the relevant strategy. This in turn may delay or prevent meeting a particular objective, with implications for reaching a certain goal. The framework makes it easy for management to track events and to predict their likely consequences.

FIGURE 7. Typical FOCUS framework results

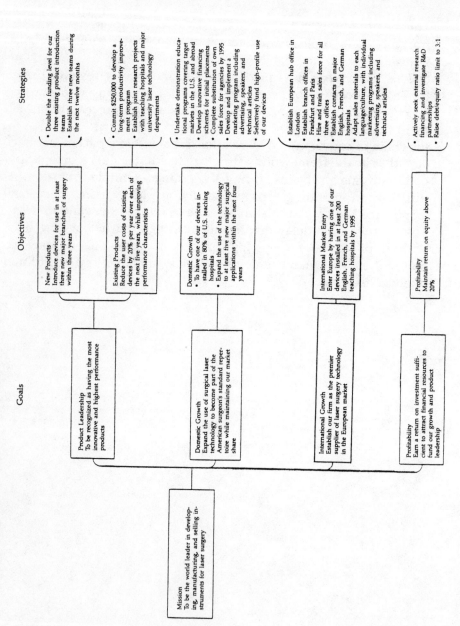

IMPLEMENTATION

The final step of strategic management is implementation. More accurately stated, implementation is not a step so much as a process—the ongoing effort to put a company's agreed-upon strategy into action, to observe its results, to review the consequences of particular choices, and to modify the strategy along the way.

Implementation is ultimately the heart of the matter. Even the best strategy will come to grief if implemented in a halfhearted, indifferent manner. Likewise, even a flawed strategy has a chance of succeeding if its proponents execute it with great vigor, observe it carefully to identify its weaknesses, and correct the problems insightfully. The goal is not theoretical perfection. Rather, the goal is a dynamic strategy that proves itself responsive to the unpredictable nature of the global marketplace.

Before proceeding with actual implementation, however, you face what you have already confronted twice before: a go/no-go decision.

You should base this decision on your answers to the following questions:

- Have you mapped out a strategy that serves your purposes, makes good use of the best information available about your target market, builds on your company's strengths, minimizes its weaknesses, and allows room for change?

- Does this strategy seem in keeping with your company's financial, human, and logistical resources?

- Is top management unified in its acceptance of and enthusiasm for the strategy—and are all the principal players involved ready to commit themselves to the time and exertion necessary for success?

- Last, is the gut-level feeling that this strategy will "fly?"

If some or all the answers to these questions are negative, then you should at least regroup and analyze what may be lacking in the strategy itself. The "no" votes may also indicate a more fundamental hesitancy to proceed with the international venture. However painful and expensive a decision to scrap the venture may be at this point, it is almost certain to be cheaper and more pleasant than proceeding into a corporate fiasco.

On the other hand, if the answers to these questions are positive, then you should proceed to the fourth and final step of going international (Step 4) or you may wish to consider further analysis by using a new tool—the Global Strategic Positioning Cube.

POSITIONING YOUR COMPANY ON THE "GLOBAL STRATEGIC POSITIONING CUBE"

The world economy has become global; resources, market opportunities, and competitive threats can be found throughout the world, especially in the key Triad areas of the Pacific Rim, North America and Europe. U.S. companies must meet foreign competition in their own backyards, and must beat foreign competitors in foreign markets. Companies that have begun to recognize this reality, and are already involved in international business operations, will gain the most from this chapter.

Global market is a frequently misunderstood and misused term. The term is often used to imply that there is one worldwide homogeneous market for a product. This is a grave mistake. Consider the United States. It is easy to see that the "U.S. market" actually consists of a number of regional markets with distinct purchasing characteristics and buyer preferences. Companies with fairly standard products adapt their product to meet regional preferences.

Companies must develop a global perspective because the opportunities and threats which exist throughout the world are interlinked. As we shall see, a company's strategy in one region, or country, can affect its performance in other regions or countries.

As stated in *The Economist* (October 18, 1989, page 78), "Global, often with an added -ising or -isation, has become one of the most over-used words of the 1980s. Yet though the idea has often been made banal, it is a problem, a challenge, and an opportunity that firms ignore at their peril."

Companies are involved in international business at different levels. In the simplest case, a company may be exporting its product

Case Study

In October, 1989, it was announced that R.H. Macy and Company agreed to allow a leading Japanese department store chain, Kintetsu, to carry Macy's private label merchandise in its ten large stores. The merchandise will include Macy's brands of clothing, linens and related goods.

The unique aspect of this agreement is that most of the merchandise will be made in the Far East, either by Macy's or by its suppliers, giving the American company an additional outlet for its large production capacity in the region. Macy's maintains a large buying office in Hong Kong that works with suppliers throughout the region. The company creates fashion designs in New York, then sends them to Asian manufacturers.

Kintetsu will benefit from lower shipping costs due to the proximity of the suppliers to Japan. The company will also enjoy the cachet of American labels, even though the clothing carrying the Macy's brand name may have been made in Asia.

Thus, Macy's original strategy of sourcing product from the Far East for the U.S. market is enabling the company to develop foreign markets. Using its established supplier base, Macy's should be able to successfully enter and compete in the Japanese market. (*The New York Times*, October 23, 1989, by Isadore Barmash.)

or sourcing part of its production without any physical (e.g., overseas office) or it may have a long-term contractual presence (e.g., joint ventures) in overseas markets. Going up the scale, a company may have established marketing joint ventures in foreign markets and set up production in others. In many cases, companies have a variety of types of relationships operating in different countries. For example, a company may have:

- A marketing joint venture to serve the Pacific Rim market;
- Regional headquarters in Brussels with hubs in a number of European countries to service the European market;

- A U.S. office that handles direct exports to individual Latin American countries;

- Sourcing arrangements with independent contractors in Hong Kong, Singapore, and Taiwan; and

- A majority interest in a *maquiladora* operation in Mexico.

It is easy to see the management nightmare created by juggling company resources among all of these locations and situations. We can see how difficult planning and decision making is for a truly global company operating throughout all major regions of the world.

To put it simply, the increased internationalization of business is making it more difficult to assess a company's position and make good decisions. There are a greater number of factors to take into account as companies do business across different cultures, time zones and political and economic systems. Companies can no longer be content with only a good sense of their competitive position in their home market. This complexity means that an assessment of one's competitive position can no longer be done without a systematic evaluation process. As Professor Etzioni wrote in a recent Harvard Business Review:

> If executives once imagined they could gather enough information to read the business environment like an open book, they have had to dim their hopes. The flow of information has swollen to such a flood that managers are in danger of drowning; extracting relevant data from the torrent is increasingly a daunting task. Little wonder that some beleaguered decision makers—even outside the White House—turn to astrologers and mediums...For example, it is no longer enough to understand the U.S. economy; events in Brazil, Kuwait, Korea, and a score of other countries are likely to affect one's decisions. (*Harvard Business Review*, July–August 1989, page 121.)

A strategic framework is necessary for companies that are going international. For the company that is already international, and must address the complexities of global business, this is even more important. Applying the strategic framework of the FOCUS method as described in pages (122–140), we can see that global business requires:

- A clear *mission* that encompasses the reality of the global market and the company's current and future position;

- *Goals* that address how the company would like to position itself in key regions and markets;
- *Objectives* that quantify these regional and country goals;
- *Strategies* that identify the opportunities to be exploited, and the resources necessary to meet the objectives and the goals; and
- *Action plans* that describe the implementation of the strategy on a product, country, and regional basis.

To develop a strategic framework in the new complex world of international business is quite difficult. For companies with limited international activities to those with extensive global operations, it is important to be able to develop and manage global strategies. To assist executives with the formation of global management strategies, I have developed a three-dimensional planning tool. This differs from the conventional two-dimensional strategy matrix. The Ernst & Young *Global Strategic Positioning Cube ("The Cube")* allows companies to assess their strengths and weaknesses in order to

- Decide where and how to focus marketing activities and overseas production ventures,
- Improve their ability to compete effectively in a variety of international markets, and
- Strengthen in-house capabilities to meet international opportunities.

As can be seen in Figure 8, the three dimensions of The Cube are:

- Strategic Importance of the Market
- Competitiveness
- In-house Capabilities

Each of these dimensions is further explained below. This is followed by some applications of The Cube. As we shall see, The Cube can be used to help a company analyze its operations in a variety of situations, and to develop ways to further exploit business opportunities.

FIGURE 8.

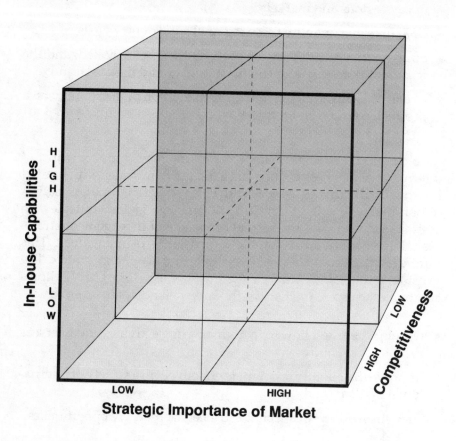

THE THREE DIMENSIONS OF THE CUBE

The Strategic Importance of the Market

The first dimension measures the strategic importance of the market to the company. This could be analyzed in a number of different ways. For example, a company could compare the strategic importance of the international market as a whole compared to the domestic market. Alternatively, it could compare the importance of individual country markets within a given region, or even worldwide.

A number of factors determine the strategic importance of a

market to a company. First, what is the size and growth of the market for the company's product? How does growth compare with other markets? What are current sales to the market? How important is this market to the total world market for the product? Finally, is the market being used, or is there a potential for use as a platform for sales to other countries (either as a marketing base or as a production base)?

Competitiveness

The second dimension compares a company's competitive position vis-à-vis its major competitors in individual markets or in the international market as a whole. Competitiveness is determined by a number of factors. First, is the product competitive in terms of price and quality? Has it been adapted and is it acceptable to local tastes and preferences? Competitiveness also takes into account the ability to market and distribute the product, to finance its sale, and to deliver it through proper logistics. In all issues, the basis of the analysis is a comparison with the company's major competitors.

In-house Capabilities

The final dimension considers a company's in-house capabilities to meet the present sales level as well as expected growth in international business. I believe that this dimension needs to be considered as it is in this area that companies often fail when it comes to international business. Commitment of management, understanding of local markets, and dedication of staff with knowledge of international business are all key factors which go into analyzing a company's in-house capabilities to meet the global challenge.

As shown in Figure 9, the losing positions within The Cube are when two or more of the dimension scores are low. Obviously, the worst case is where all three dimensions are low, or in the lower-left-back position. In the case illustrated, for example, in Figure 9, the company already has a competitive product, and is thus in the lower-left-front octant.

The U.S. Academic Response to Globalization

The American academic community has realized in recent years that American students have not been sufficiently prepared to meet the challenges of international business. In response, programs have been developed to train students in those skills required for successful international marketing. For example, the Wharton School at the University of Pennsylvania has a program to train MBA candidates in multinational business. The Fletcher School of Law and Diplomacy, the nation's first school of international affairs, has a separate international business program. The University of South Carolina offers a Masters degree in International Business Studies. Even the McLean, Virginia *high school* system recently instituted a pilot program in international trade. These are just a few examples of the educational programs now being offered in international business which should improve the in-house capabilities of firms to compete in the global market in the decades to come.

FIGURE 9.

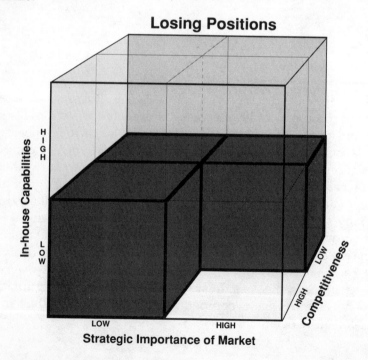

The objective for companies is to move away from these losing positions to a winning position. For example, a company found in the lower-left-front of The Cube, as in Figure 9, would want to take action to (1) improve its in-house capabilities and (2) move to more strategically important markets. The company would then end up in a winning position, as shown in Figures 10 and 11.

The Winning Position

Many U.S. companies have succeeded in achieving and maintaining the winning position in their global, regional, and country markets. They have targeted the strategically important markets, developed a high competitive position and cultivated in-house capabilities. I present a few examples of these companies:

Coca Cola.   Coca Cola has succeeded in developing international markets for its products. Through advertising and other methods, the company has successfully penetrated markets throughout the

FIGURE 10.

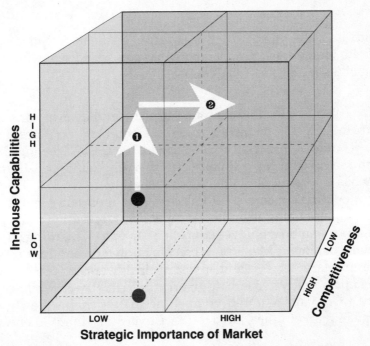

FIGURE 11.

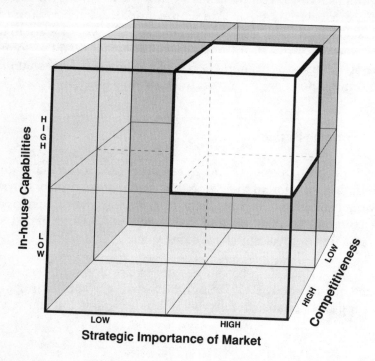

world. Its willingness to try innovative business techniques has facilitated its success. This company has developed strong in-house capabilities for international business.

IBM. IBM is the leading computer firm in virtually every one of the approximately 130 countries where the company operates. IBM's biggest strength is its skill at blending marketing and technical considerations to come up with products that sell. To this end, the company has a worldwide intelligence gathering network to keep up with events in its markets. IBM places equal importance in developing and maintaining its in-house capabilities, spending millions of dollars per year on employee education. As part of guarding its competitive position, IBM has been cracking down on entities that steal its proprietary secrets, and investing in lower-cost producers to maintain its ability to compete on price. IBM has the capabilities and savvy to remain a tough competitor in the challenging global computer market. (*Time*, July 11, 1983, Cover Story, John Greenwald.)

McDonald's.   McDonald's has franchised its business throughout the world but maintains consistent quality by training managers and employees in the United States. McDonald's carefully selects its overseas partners so that it can allow local management to take the lead. The company sources locally, and maintains its edge over the competition by modifying its product, marketing, and advertising for the local culture. In Hong Kong, McDonald's has some of the highest transaction counts of any of the chain's restaurants worldwide, helped by give-aways of Muppet Baby toys and miniature dragons, in observance of the Year of the Dragon. McDonald's has been so successful in its assimilation in different cultures, that a first-time visitor to the United States from Japan commented that he felt right at home in America—after all, "They have McDonald's, too."

APPLICATIONS OF THE CUBE

The Cube can be used to analyze a company's position on a number of different levels. The Cube can be used:

- To analyze a company's global position
- To assess a company's position in different regions
- To analyze and compare a company's position among individual countries

An application of The Cube for each of these uses is presented below. I have simplified the analysis by having only two possible scores—high and low. It is clear that there are gradations within these extremes that need to be considered in more complex analyses.

TABLE 2.   Analyzing a Company's Global Position

Example 1—CompanyA	
	Score
Strategic Importance of Market	High
Competitivenes	Low
In-house Capabilities	Low

All of Company A's major competitors have witnessed rapid growth in export sales in recent years. While Company A's exports have grown, they have done so at a lower rate than their competitors'.

Company A is weak in several areas of its competitive position. For example, it has had trouble adapting its product for international markets, and it has not established a good overseas network. Its primary competitors have offices in all of the key country markets, while Company A is still servicing these markets through a distribution network of manufacturer's reps and agents overseas. Because of this, the company has a low competitive position. In addition, Company A's in-house capabilities for international business are weak: there is no strong management commitment (in spite of the growing sales potential), and few experienced staff dedicated to international sales.

Company A falls into the lower-back-right octant of The Cube. As has been clearly demonstrated, the international market is of high strategic importance. The company should take actions to place itself in a better position to exploit this potential. It must:

- Improve its competitive position (moving forward in The Cube). This could be done through better management of its overseas representatives and agents or by establishing an overseas office.

- Improve its in-house capabilities (moving upward in The Cube) through actions such as hiring additional staff with international expertise and dedicating more senior management time to global planning and oversight.

By undertaking these steps the company will end up in the winning position (the upper-right-front of The Cube), as shown in Figure 12.

TABLE 3. Comparing Regional Positions

Example 2—Company B		
	Score	
	Pacific Rim	Europe
Strategic Importance of Market	High	High
Competitiveness	High	Low
In-house Capabilities	Low	High

FIGURE 12.

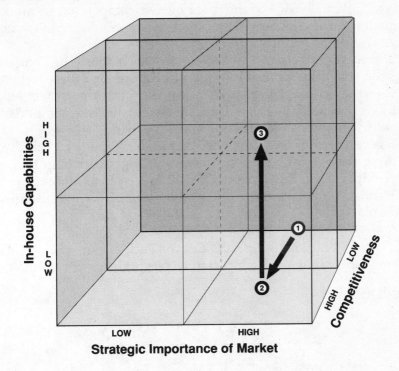

Company B has decided to evaluate its position in two regions of the Triad—the Pacific Rim and Europe. The company recognizes that both areas are strategically very important. Europe represents a huge market, and the company will have opportunities to expand its sales from the few countries it is presently operating in. While sales to the Pacific Rim are lower than European sales, the company knows that as the economies of the region develop, there will be great demand for its product. The company has also been sourcing some components from the region, and is considering establishing a joint venture to ensure access to further supply. In addition, the company is aware that its principal competitors have been expanding operations in the region, and believe that they must meet this competition head on.

On the dimension of competitiveness, the company is in a better position in the Pacific Rim than it is in Europe. The company has successfully adapted its product in a number of Asian markets, and has excellent distributors in the region. In Europe, in spite of extensive efforts, the company has not been as successful in marketing its product, partially due to the more intense competition from local companies. The company therefore scores high in competitiveness in Asia and low in Europe.

The scores are reversed on in-house capabilities. The company has been focusing more of its efforts on Europe, and there has been little management commitment to further developing the Asian market. The company has replaced its recently retired staff of Asian experts with personnel with European experience.

Figure 13 summarizes the position of the company in The Cube. In Asia, the company is in the lower-front-right corner. In Europe, the company is in the upper-back-right corner. To optimize its position in both markets and to take advantage of the importance of these markets the company must do the following:

- Improve its in-house capabilities for Pacific Rim business. The company might want to hire staff with experience in the region, or

FIGURE 13.

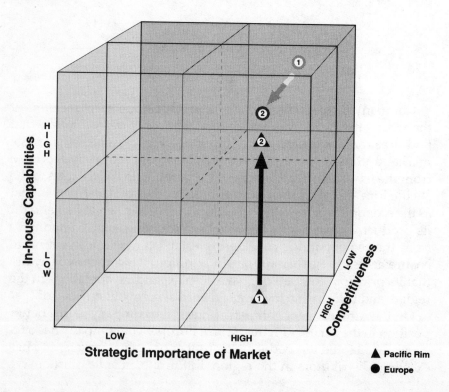

send existing staff to training programs. Management must show increased commitment to developing this business.

- Improve its competitive position in Europe. The company needs to spend more time studying and implementing ways to improve its product acceptance in the market. The company must also expand its presence in the market to better compete with European companies. The company might even want to consider a joint venture to be able to effectively cover all of Europe.

By undertaking these actions, the company will be able to move to the winning position in The Cube, the upper-front-right position.

TABLE 4. Comparison Among Countries

| | Example 3—Company C | | | |
| | Score | | | |
	FRG	France	Sweden	Holland
Strategic Importance of Market	High	High	Low	Low
Competitiveness	High	Low	High	Low
In-house Capabilities	Low	Low	Low	Low

In the third example I evaluate Company C's position in four country markets in Europe. Both West Germany and France are strategically important markets to the company. Sweden and Holland, on the other hand, are relatively small, unimportant markets for Company C, though its products are competitive there. The company has a strong competitive position in the important West Germany market, where it has a major office. In France, the company is in a weak competitive position in a market it considers important and in which it has low in-house capabilities. Company C does not have an office in France and its current distributor does not have the financial resources to undertake sales efforts.

The company's in-house capabilities are generally low. Management has shown limited commitment to international business, and there is insufficient staff to even maintain current business. There is little awareness of the importance of international business throughout the company except from the international business manager. This has affected the performance of the overseas distributors who do not feel they receive enough support from the company.

Based upon this analysis, the company's priority actions should be:

- Improve its in-house capabilities for international business as this is affecting its abilities in all markets. The chief executives need to demonstrate their commitment to international business. This could include more frequent visits to overseas offices, distributors, and representatives.

- Improve its competitive position in France, as this represents a market of high strategic importance. The company should try to find a new distributor who can meet the objectives established by the company. Alternatively, the company might want to consider opening an office in France. This office could report directly to U.S. headquarters.

- A low priority action would be to improve the company's competitive situation in Holland as the market is not of high strategic importance.

- There is no need to take action in Sweden. The company is in a strong competitive position in a small market.

Figure 14 shows how all of these operations are currently positioned and the effect of carrying out all of the foregoing actions.

POSITIONING YOUR COMPANY

The following exercise will help you to identify where your company is positioned in the Global Strategic Positioning Cube.

There is a set of five questions for each of the dimensions of the Global Cube. Points are given for each of the questions and an average

FIGURE 14.

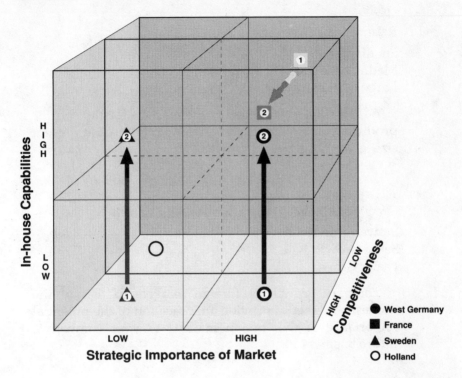

score is derived for each of the dimensions. Obviously, this questionnaire allows only a quick analysis of the company's position. However, we believe that this is a good first step to analyze a company's position in the global marketplace. Each of the questions could be evaluated in-depth to assess the true situation of your company.

As shown in the above examples, The Cube can be used to analyze a number of different aspects of a company's global position. Obviously, the answers to the questions need to be tailored to reflect the different levels each company places on each of the attributes. At the end of the exercise, Figure 15 gives an example of The Cube for plotting your company's position using your score on the questions.

I. STRATEGIC IMPORTANCE OF MARKET

I.1 *Relative Size of Market*

Small market	=	0
Medium market	=	5
Large market	=	10

Address the overall size of the markets for the specific products you are considering, taking into account present size as well as expected growth.

I.2 *Growth of Market Compared to Domestic Market*

Slower growth	=	0
Same Growth	=	5
Faster Growth	=	10

Compare growth of foreign markets to that of the domestic market to provide an indication of the potential importance of the foreign markets to your company's future business.

I.3 *Importance of Market to Total World Market*

Low	=	0
Medium	=	5
High	=	10

Evaluate how important the particular market is to the overall world market for your product.

I.4 *Current Sales to Market*

Insignificant	=	0
Medium importance	=	5
Very important	=	10

If sales to the market represent a significant portion of your company's overall sales, the market is obviously of greater strategic importance.

I.5 *Present Use of, or Potential to Use of Market as Base for Sales to Other Countries*

Low	=	0
Medium	=	5
High	=	10

Consider whether the market is being used, or has the potential to be used, as a platform for sales to other countries. For example: an overseas office which could manage sales to neighboring countries; or an overseas production facility which could supply product to other countries in the region.

Now add all the individual scores up and enter them below and perform the averaging calculation, as indicated.

SCORE =   _____
Divide by 5
AVERAGE SCORE =   _____

Plot the average score on The Cube in Figure 15 on the axis entitled "Strategic Importance of Market".

II. COMPETITIVENESS

II.1 Price/Performance Ratio

Worse than competitors	=	0
Equal to competitors	=	5
Better than competitors	=	10

Evaluate how your company's product compares in price and quality with your competitor's products. Consider this question on a market-by-market basis. The impact of exchange rates on prices needs to be considered.

II.2 Product Acceptance in Market

Worse than competitors	=	0
Equal to competitors	=	5
Better than competitors	=	10

In addition to the standard price and quality issues addressed in question II.1, it is important to consider how well your product is accepted in the local market. This would also include compliance with local technical standards. In most cases, some adaptation, at the least in packaging, will be necessary. This is a key competitive factor that is often overlooked.

II.3 Marketing, Sales, and Promotion in Foreign Market

Worse than competitors	= 0
Equal to competitors	= 5
Better than competitors	= 10

Compare your company with its competitors in ability to effectively market and promote a product in the foreign market. In cases where you use distributors, focus on the capabilities of the distributors and your ability to effectively manage and support these distributors. If your company uses its own local office, or sells directly through headquarters, the evaluation must focus on internal abilities.

II.4 Distribution and Transportation for Foreign Market

Worse than competitors	= 0
Equal to competitors	= 5
Better than competitors	= 10

Consider how your company distributes and transports its products to foreign markets. Is the product being delivered on time in the most cost effective way? Have you established an efficient warehousing and distribution system within the region or country?

II.5 Financial Strength for International Business

Worse than competitors	= 0
Equal to competitors	= 5
Better than competitors	= 10

Address your company's financial strength to support international business. Can the company finance its export sales either internally or through external public or private sources? Is there sufficient capital to establish an overseas office or plant or the means of raising capital when the time comes for expansion?

SCORE =   _____
Divide by 5
AVERAGE SCORE =   _____

Now take the average score and plot it on the axis entitled "Competitiveness" in Figure 15.

III.   IN-HOUSE CAPABILITIES

III.1 Staff Dedicated to International Business

Inadequate for present level of business	= 0
Adequate for present level of business	= 5
Adequate flexibility for increasing business	= 10

Examine your present level of staffing and how it relates to the level of international business. Is there adequate staff to handle the existing level of business in the particular market or region? Would there be adequate staff if there were a significant increase in international sales?

III.2 Company's Expertise in Export Finance and Logistics

Low	= 0
Medium	= 5
High	= 10

Assess your company's internal expertise in the mechanics of international trade and trade finance. Can your company effectively handle tariffs, custom procedures, export documentation, letters of credit, Eximbank financing, and so forth? Evaluate general capabilities as well as those applicable to the specific markets or regions being analyzed.

III. 3 Company's Expertise in International Marketing

Low	=	0
Medium	=	5
High	=	10

Assess your expertise in international marketing for the markets being considered. How well do you understand the distribution system, the role of advertising and promotion, and the purchasing habits of buyers in foreign markets?

III. 4 Commitment of Management and Willingness to Commit Resources

Low	=	0
Medium	=	5
High	=	10

Weigh the commitment of management to the market. Your company's overall commitment to international business as well as commitment to particular markets need to be considered. Commitment, or lack of it, can manifest itself in different forms. Does the president of the company spend time in overseas markets? How much resources are dedicated to exploring new international markets? Are staff members actively encouraged to become aware of the important role of international business?

III. 5 Understanding of Local Market Including Competitor's Activities

Weak	=	0
Fair	=	5
Strong	=	10

The final consideration in this dimension is your company's understanding of your competitor's activities in the region or country being analyzed. It would be unthinkable for a U.S. company not to know what its competitors are doing in the U.S., yet many companies cannot even tell you who their competitors are in overseas markets. For the more sophisticated company, it is important to understand competitor's activities and strategies in order to be able to effectively compete. This question measures your ability to do that.

SCORE =   _____
Divide by 5
AVERAGE SCORE =   _____

Now take the average score from here and enter it on the "In-house Capabilities" axis of The Cube below and you will now be able to see how your company is positioned.

If you ranked yourself low in competitive position or in-house capabilities, you need to establish ways to

FIGURE 15.

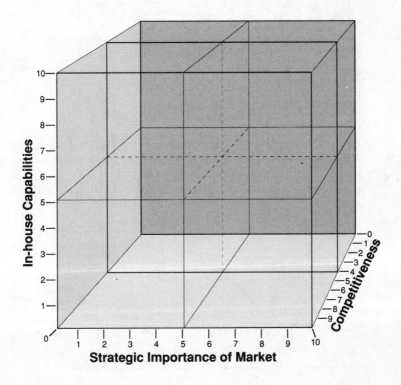

improve your situation. Go back to the questions and carefully evaluate why you scored low. Actions need to be taken to remedy these shortcomings. If you are in markets of low strategic importance, then consider refocusing your marketing efforts on markets of greater strategic importance.

IN CONCLUSION

Obviously, analyzing your company on The Cube is an extensive process, and requires more than the cursory treatment given above. However, the key factors that must be considered are the same. I believe that you can use the questionnaire and apply as much depth as necessary to each of the questions to determine where your company is, and where it could and should be.

Case Study

PRI Industries, a $20 million high-tech manufacturer located in the northeast, initially gave little attention to the export market, and "looked at export orders like some kind of gift from heaven." A few years ago it decided to be more pro-active in seeking sales overseas. The company judged that foreign markets were growing in strategic importance. PRI appointed an international sales manager to develop and train distributors in Europe. He found that all the sales prospects and distributors he met with spoke excellent English, and he felt that not knowing any foreign languages was no serious disadvantage. After two years, however, results were disappointing, even though the company was convinced it had the best product on the market and it was price-competitive.

While still trying to develop an effective export marketing strategy, the company received an opportunity to bid on a $250,000 order from a well known major German manufacturing concern (BMM). This opportunity was viewed as a sort of test by the company's management, and they decided to go all out to win. The company's product was short-listed, and the international

---

Case Study (Continued)

sales manager made the final presentation to BMM's selection committee.

After the presentation, the international sales manager telephoned the head office back in the United States. The top executives were confidently expecting to be told that they had won the order. Instead, they were shocked to hear the following story:

The BMM committee listened attentively to the presentation and seemed very interested in the product. Eventually the chief engineer said, in perfect English, "Thank you for an excellent presentation. I think you have an outstanding product. Do you have a technical manual that you can show us?" The sales manager pulled one from his briefcase and handed it to him, saying, "Of course. I think you'll be very impressed by the quality of our technical documentation." The chief engineer also asked for copies of the operator's manual and the price list for parts and supplies. All of these were comprehensive, well designed, and attractively packaged—in fact, they were often a real selling point in themselves for the company in the United States.

After examining the documentation for a few minutes, the chief engineer stood up, faced the sales manager, and spoke very bluntly. "You Americans are so arrogant. You ask us to rely on your machine for a vital part of our new project. We have to train our operators. We have to learn to maintain your machine and keep the required parts on hand. But all these manuals are in English. Our workers cannot understand them. Your price list is in dollars, 'FOB New York.' Who is going to pay the freight, the duty, the insurance? No. We will not buy your machine."

At first the executives in the United States were outraged by this reaction. Eventually, however, they realized that the Germans were absolutely right, and had in fact done them a big favor.

In terms of The Cube, the company's European strategic position could be scored as follows:

Case Study (Continued)

STRATEGIC IMPORTANCE		COMPETITIVENESS		IN-HOUSE CAPABILITIES	
Relative Size of Market	10	Price Performance	10	Dedicated Staff	0
Growth of Market	10	Product Acceptance	5	Expertise in International Marketing	5
Current Sales	5	Marketing/Sales/Promotion	0	Expertise in Finance	5
Importance to World Market	10	Distribution & Transportation	5	Commitment	0
Use as Base	10	Financial Strength	5	Understanding International Marketing	0
SUM	45		25		10
Divide by 5					
SCORE	9		5		2

The company realized that they would have to improve both their competitive position and their in-house capabilities if they were going to compete in Europe. To do so, they felt that it would have to be as a European firm. The company established a European office in the United Kingdom, and even purchased its own building there. The company worked at adapting its products, translating its sales literature and documentation, and seeking out the right sales representatives in target countries. All of these actions greatly improved their competitiveness.

Management demonstrated an increased commitment to international business, more staff were dedicated, and the company spent a year in careful study of international markets. Thus, their in-house capabilities were greatly improved.

As a result, the company was ready to enter both the German and French markets. The company was able to move itself in the Cube into the winning position, as shown in Figure 16.

FIGURE 16.

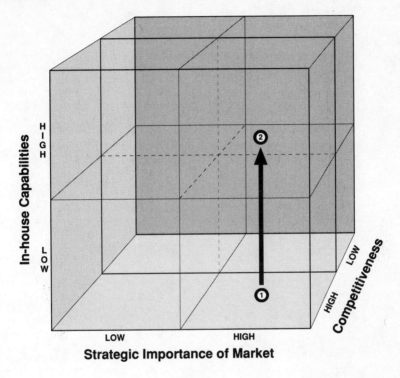

STEP 4 _____

BEATING THEM AT THEIR OWN GAME

Now comes the most difficult, but at the same time, the most potentially rewarding phase of going international.

You have tested the waters, learned the language, and mapped out a strategy. You have decided at each step that you have good reason to expand your operations into the global marketplace, and you have consequently made the necessary commitments of time, money, and personnel. You are ready to confront your competitors—and ready to beat them at their own game.

What are the final aspects of starting to do business abroad? What should you keep in mind as you proceed to establish your niche, make sales, reap profits, and attain whatever other goals you have set out to accomplish?

The sections that follow—unlike those preceding—are not a unified sequence of tasks. Rather, Step 4 is a survey of several important issues that U. S. companies too often ignore, neglect, or leave to last-minute improvisation. By considering these issues and determining how they may affect your international venture, you can avoid some potential problems and increase your chances for success overseas.

THE RULES OF THE GAME

On the most basic level, beating your competitors at their own game means implementing the strategy already mapped out during the third step of going international. Specifically, you must execute the action plans that constitute your strategy in its most detailed form; you must track the results of these action plans in both quantitative and qualitative terms; and you must take the results into consideration as part of the iterative process of strategic management. But you must, in addition, pay attention to the fundamental rules of doing business abroad.

These rules are as follows:

- *Commit the best available personnel to your international venture.* To beat the competition, you need people who are dedicated to the company and committed to understanding a new culture and a new market. The higher the quality of your officers (and the longer-term their commitment to the venture), the better the chances of their developing the contacts, personal relationships, and knowledge necessary for success.

- *Be flexible.* No matter how westernized the modern world may seem, cultural differences still run deep. Doing business in Beijing, Riyadh, Paris, or even London often bears little resemblance to doing business in Seattle, Dallas, Nashville, or Boston. Beating the competition means playing by local rules.

- *Above all, stay patient.* Your competitors will feel they have time on their side. In Asia, businesses routinely plan ten to twenty years in advance. In Europe, ten-year time horizons are common. Your commitment must be substantial, durable, and confident. Only those who play for the long haul will win.

Beating your competitors at their own game also means keeping a close watch on four issues that companies sidestep only at their own peril. Specifically, you should pay special attention to:

1. Selecting and dealing with expatriates,
2. Training personnel in cross-cultural skills,
3. Considering special tips for success, and
4. Avoiding common pitfalls.

SELECTING AND DEALING WITH EXPATRIATES

Some companies set up successful overseas operations without employing an expatriate field staff. Frequent telecommunications with local representatives plus periodic trips abroad allow some corporate officers to manage their ventures essentially by remote control. In theory, there is nothing wrong with such arrangements; in practice, they often prove successful. Moreover, this method offers the advantage of being less expensive than methods involving an expatriate field staff.

However, three major benefits accrue from having expatriates in your overseas office, benefits so significant and substantial that they should not be overlooked.

1. Having an expatriate field officer allows you to monitor operations far better than you would be able to otherwise.
2. Having an expatriate field officer simplifies the task of dealing with other American companies overseas, since the executives of these other firms may prefer to deal with fellow countrymen.
3. An expatriate field officer will presumably come from one of your existing domestic operations, and thus will know and understand your company culture, will already have established relationships with key executives in your home office, and will be experienced in your company's procedures.

The main goals of maintaining an expatriate presence in your overseas office are *monitoring* and *control* of the business environment. And the experience of many U.S. corporations suggests overwhelmingly that monitoring and control are more easily accomplished with an expatriate officer on site.

Sitting at a desk back home, you may find it difficult to interpret events in your overseas markets, no matter how closely you follow developments in foreign periodicals or company reports. Is your local rep energetically and accurately representing the firm to host-country clients? Or is he neglecting his commitment to you, perhaps making an effort only when you fly out for a visit? Your long-distance vantage point may leave you with an overly optimistic impression of how you're doing overseas.

Alternatively, the view from headquarters may distort your perceptions in the opposite direction. Is the rep actually working *harder* than sales figures would suggest? Is the task of getting yourself established in the target market more complicated than you first thought? If you feel frustrated by your sense of the rep's work so far, are you perhaps underestimating the difficulties he faces in doing business in the host country?

Whether the overall situation is going better or worse than you anticipated, you'll have a hard time knowing the reality of the matter without your own staffer in the field. By contrast, with a member of your home team overseas, you can learn more directly how your product sells, how your service team performs, how your clients react, and how other aspects of going international take shape. You can stay in tune with developments in market penetration, competitors' activities, political and economic risk, changes in the infrastructure, and so forth.

Expats—The Biggest Asset, The Biggest Problem

For these reasons, expats are your biggest asset in going international. You have your own person on the scene; you receive direct feedback. Your field officer speaks your corporate language, so you don't have to worry about the communication problems. He or she can provide you with the clearest insight into your foreign market short of spending your own time there at length. In short, expats are invaluable.

At the same time, expatriates are also the biggest problem. Expats can be demanding, unpredictable, or eccentric. Some grow more and more obsessive about their salaries or benefits. Some develop personal problems in the course of adjusting to another culture. Marital difficulties, depression, and alcoholism can develop among hastily selected, ill-prepared expats. A small minority of expats either can't adjust to life overseas at all or else adjust far too well and "go native."

(A brief aside about "going native." This term refers to the phenomenon in which someone stationed overseas takes on the customs, attitudes, and other attributes of the host-country populace. It isn't simply a question of cultural adaptation. Learning about and respecting the local customs is, of course, desirable and necessary. However, some expatriates make such complete adjustments that in some sense they cease to be expatriates at all. The problem here is not that your field officer now eats different food or wears different clothing. Rather, the problem is that if this person now chooses to do business in the host-country manner, or to follow the local time sense, or to hold the host-country values, your company ceases to have an "inside person" at all. You are now dealing with yet another outsider.)

Despite these risks, however, expatriates are worth the trouble to find, train, and place in overseas posts. Most carefully selected, well-prepared expats adjust to their foreign assignments and perform successfully. They learn the language, settle into their new roles, and thrive in unfamiliar environments. In short, expats are a tricky issue but often a major advantage in an international venture.

Financial Issues

Expatriates are expensive. You should be prepared to deal with a variety of costs from the outset:

- Salary
- Overseas premium
- Cost-of-living adjustments (from the city of origin to destination)
- Hardship or hazardous assignment pay (in a host country subject to political instability, military conflict, or other contingencies)
- Housing allowances
- Income tax adjustments
- Moving expenses and set-up costs

- Local transportation costs (company car, sometimes with driver included)
- Schooling for the employee's children
- Home leave for the family
- Emergency and compassionate leave (for a death or illness in the family)
- Medical leave

Estimating a specific dollar cost for these items requires a knowledge of each country. As a rough estimate, however, you can figure that an employee on assignment overseas will cost you between three and five times his or her U.S. salary plus benefits. The specifics of particular packages vary significantly. Banks and oil companies offer expatriates more generous packages than smaller private corporations. To attract and retain high caliber expatriates, you must offer terms that are at least competitive with typical middle-range packages; otherwise you may end up with an employee who spends most of his or her time unhappy with himself or herself, with the company, and with life in general. Ultimately, as the level of misery increases and productivity drops, the underpaid expat will cost you more than a well-chosen, properly paid employee would have in the first place.

Who Are You Looking For?

Identifying the ideal candidate for an overseas post is generally not a simple matter. Suppose you intend to open up an Indonesian distribution network. By luck, your vice president for marketing is a bright, energetic, flexible world traveler who revels in cultural diversity, learns easily, and just happens to speak fluent Javanese, Bahasa Indonesia, and Dutch. Without a doubt you've found your ideal employee. But this scenario is unlikely to the point of fantasy. More likely, you have a pool of candidates who are talented executives but who lack many of the skills that would ensure a perfect match. Who's the best bet? And what sorts of backgrounds should you look for as you pick and choose?

In addition to fundamental qualifications, these are the most important criteria for the potential expatriate officer:

- *Overall job performance.* High achievement in service to the company is, of course, the fundamental criterion for an expatriate field officer. Only first-rate employees will thrive in their new environment. The ideal candidate must fully understand the company's goals in going international, yet at the same time must be a highly motivated self-starter.

- *Past success overseas.* A candidate who has worked well overseas—even in a culture far different from your current target market—is a better bet than one who has never experienced the task of adjusting to another country.

- *Flexibility.* Since an overseas assignment will invariably present the expat with a new, different, and initially confusing cultural environment, a flexible attitude toward people and situations is a big plus.

- *Patience.* "Time-is-money" fanatics will have severe difficulties in most countries—and will frustrate host-country customers and business partners as well. Someone who is energetic but also aware of other people's time sense will get more done than a compulsive watch-tapper.

- *Sense of humor.* A candidate who seems unable or unwilling to laugh at the sometimes bumpy road to adjustment in another country is doomed to failure. Anyone who *can* laugh at cross-cultural adventures—or who *enjoys* laughing—will have a far easier time in the first place.

- *Marital and family stability.* Overseas assignments are often rough not just on the expat, but on the spouse and children as well. A rocky marriage will get rockier; unhappy children will end up still unhappier. The family's state of mind will heavily influence the expat's success or failure as much as his or her own abilities and attitudes as an employee.

- *An ability to handle stress.* Although many people find overseas work to be stimulating, even exhilarating, the initial adjustment is always emotionally stressful. Some posts will be physically stressful as well, depending on the climate, standard of living, and so forth. Finally, most people go through *culture shock*, the often confusing experience of adapting to another way of life.

What sorts of assessments can you make from these guidelines? That depends on the particular job, particular host country, and particular candidate. A promising candidate would be a flexible, open-minded person, ideally with some sort of previous experience in living overseas, whose spouse is supportive of the opportunity to live in another country. (From a cost standpoint, a candidate with few or no children is generally preferable to one with a larger family.) To some extent, single candidates may be more promising than married candidates.

People to avoid at all costs are the escapee, the total unknown, and the mercenary.

The Escapee. Watch out for candidates whose reason for going overseas is to escape something—a dead-end career, a sense of personal failure, or a bad marriage. Some people imagine that an overseas post will resemble a vacation in Tahiti. The shock of the actual situation has cost U.S. companies untold millions. Still more common are the people who expect a new setting to solve their marital problems, only to discover that even a satisfying post can further strain a shaky marriage.

The Total Unknown. Hiring someone from outside your company is also risky. You want someone who has worked in your organization for years—someone who knows the company culture, believes in the company values, and strives for the company well-being. If you feel tempted to hire an outsider, imagine the potential risks of having an unfamiliar officer reporting from unfamiliar territory, thus compounding all your uncertainties about what goes on in the field.

The Mercenary. Mercenaries don't want the job because the work challenges and interests them, or because the position contributes to their career path. They just want it for the money. If the expat's *sole* concern is money, then career advancement, pride in personal achievement, and the firm itself are ultimately of little consequence. The mercenary is merely a corporate soldier of fortune exploiting the company.

The Spouse—The Most Frequently Overlooked Variable

In the past, many American companies focused only on the candidate for an overseas position and neglected a critical variable: the candidate's spouse. The spouse is as likely to determine the expat's success or failure as the expat himself or herself.

Consequently, U.S. firms are now tending to interview the candidate's spouse at the same time as the candidate. Moreover, in an increasing number of instances, companies arrange for a prospective expatriate officer *and* the spouse to visit the foreign post, spend a few weeks there, and get a feel for the host country firsthand. (Some companies limit these visits to a week; ideally, however, the visit should extend to at least two weeks. A shorter visit complicates the task of getting an accurate sense of the place and the local culture.) During these visits, the expat and the spouse spend time with other Americans, see the stores, visit the schools, and tour local residences. Although costly, these test visits generally prevent the far greater expense of hiring an expat whose spouse or family ends up unhappy, thus resulting in an abortive assignment.

The Expat Career Path

The final and critical consideration when dealing with expats is the career path. In the past, some American companies used foreign posts as places to send their misfits and has-beens. These companies tended to make their international divisions the corporate equivalent of Siberia. By no means all employees posted overseas were misfits and has-beens. Some were, however. As a result, receiving an overseas assignment subjected even first-rate, highly committed employees to questions like "They're sending you to the boonies?" and "What have you done wrong?"

Fortunately, the situation is now changing. Top management is understanding the importance of the international sector in its own right. But U.S. firms still have some distance to go in defining the expat career path as something that is not merely tolerable, but desirable as well.

To make overseas posts truly attractive to the company's most talented employees, you should build the importance of international ventures into the company culture itself. The message to employees should be the following:

- *To attain top management positions, middle managers must go overseas at some point in their careers.* A foreign assignment is crucial for them to understand and value the firm's international commitments and projects. International work is important and will become increasingly important in the future.

- *The officer who takes an overseas post is not being put out to pasture.* On the contrary, he or she is undertaking a critical aspect of the company's work.

- *All employees who go overseas are guaranteed a position with the firm afterward.* This doesn't mean that top management will write a contract guaranteeing the employee a particular job for a particular period upon his or her return from the foreign post; you do, however, want to build into the corporate culture a perception that going international is a desirable, creative path within the company.

To foster these perceptions, you should build a roster of people within the company who have served overseas, who have returned to the domestic office or offices, and who are now in leadership positions. Such changes in company culture are more a question of top management's attitudes than of specific provisions. The message to all talented managers should be: "Going overseas means that you are an important person within this company. We trust you. By letting you have the unprecedented amount of responsibility in the overseas office—responsibility that we wouldn't give to most people—we're preparing you for a greater leadership position when you return."

In the final analysis, you should pick your staff members for overseas assignments not just because you want *them* to believe this message, but because you believe it yourself. If you assign personnel to overseas posts just because you don't know what to do with them otherwise, or because they are problematic and you want them out of your sight, you're making a mistake. If your employee isn't succeeding in the United States, he or she certainly won't succeed overseas. Only the most dynamic, adaptable, and tenacious individuals succeed.

TRAINING PERSONNEL IN CROSS-CULTURAL SKILLS

Although the executives most likely to succeed overseas are those who are already successful at home, excellence here is *in itself* no guarantee of excellence there. Other factors contribute to the quality of performance in another culture: language skills, personal resilience, cultural sensitivity, and knowledge about the host country. Fortunately, qualified candidates for overseas posts can augment their qualifications through well-chosen cross-cultural training, which will in turn increase the chances for beating the competition at their own game.

Every business person going overseas should take a course in cross-cultural training specific to the host country or region. Experience in dealing with other nations is, of course, helpful. But countries differ from each other in such numerous and often dramatic ways that nothing can truly replace detailed information, advice, and coaching from knowledgeable sources. The cost of such training is often high; however, cross-cultural training almost always pays off in heightened confidence and new insights. Such confidence and insight will ultimately contribute to the bottom line.

Sources of Information and Assistance

You can obtain cross-cultural training from a variety of sources. The most common types of organizations that provide cross-cultural training are the following:

- Cross-cultural training specialists
- International management consultants
- Accounting firms
- Universities and business schools
- Some large language-instruction firms

In addition, some banks and CPA firms in the host country may offer short courses about business customs in that setting.

Another source of information—useful both before and during an overseas assignment—is books about general or specific cultural issues. One of the best general guides is *Going International: How to Make Friends and Deal Effectively in the Global Marketplace* by Lennie Copeland and Lewis Griggs (Random House, 1985). (Copeland and Griggs have also produced a series of audio and video tapes by the same title.) More specific guides to individual cultures include various series with titles like *Doing Business in [Country]*, with separate volumes focusing on nations throughout Europe, Asia, and the Middle East. Note, however, that books are probably an insufficient means of orientation before an overseas assignment. More interactive, in-person coaching is a necessary complement to even the most thorough reading program.

What Helps—and How It Helps

The fact is, the better prepared your expatriate officer is upon arrival in the host country, the more quickly and easily that person will be able to adjust, to work efficiently, and to accomplish the company's goals. Certain specific components of cross-cultural training can make the whole process simpler and more successful for everyone concerned. The most critical of these components are the following:

- *Language training.* Learning the host country's native language is often the most crucial dimension of cross-cultural training, though of course the specific circumstances depend on the country in question. Generally speaking, the expat should start language lessons, even in relatively accessible languages (such as Spanish or French), at least several months before departure. Learning non-Western languages like Japanese, Thai, or Chinese requires far longer, more intensive effort.

- *Cultural orientation.* Expatriates who understand how people live in the host country will adjust far more easily than those who arrive unsure of what to expect. Personal etiquette, time sense, formalities, and other local customs are all far easier to grasp if they don't come as a complete surprise.

- *National or regional history.* Although relatively unimportant to many expats, local history is the focal point of so many misunderstandings that all Americans traveling overseas would benefit from a wider historical background. The resulting advantage isn't just more knowledge of why people do what they do and believe what they believe. In addition, host-country business partners and customers take the expat's knowledge of their history as a compliment, and often respond more openly as a result.

- *Religious issues*. The same holds true for knowledge of religious customs, including holidays, taboos, dietary issues, and any factional, regional, or international disputes.

- *Lifestyle issues*. What sorts of houses do people live in? What kinds of food do they eat? How, when, and where do they shop? What side of the road do they drive on? These and other questions get at the lifestyle issues that make the details of daily living different from one culture to another.

In dealing with these various dimensions of another culture, the goal is *not* to identify every difference, to learn every custom, or to anticipate every difficulty. Such a goal would be unattainable, and perhaps undesirable as well. Rather, the goal is to gain an overall sense of the culture that the expat will encounter, and to some extent to identify easily avoided problem areas. Nothing totally prepares an expat for either the challenges or the delights of experiencing a new culture. Cross-cultural training can, however, make the challenges less difficult and the delights more obvious.

DIFFERENCES IN INDUSTRIAL RELATIONS

Companies often enter business overseas without giving consideration to the cost of local hires. A common misconception is that local hires are cheaper than hiring and producing in the United States. This is because companies focus only on basic wage rates, a measure that is deceptive. It is also important to take into account benefit costs and the productivity of the work force.

Benefit costs vary dramatically from country to country. As shown in Table 5, benefit costs range from 20 percent of wages (Hong Kong) to 100 percent of wages (Japan).

Some companies also only consider the costs of labor without considering the productivity. This is a mistake. For example, labor in Central America is less expensive than in Hong Kong, Taiwan, and Korea. Yet companies that have relocated their production to

Central America have generally found that the low productivity of labor can erode the benefits from lower costs.

TABLE 5. Benefit Costs as a Percentage of Wages
(selected countries)

Country	Benefit (%)	Hourly Wages U.S.$ (1989)	Total Hourly Costs
West Germany	83	17.53	32.08
Sweden	46	17.48	25.52
Japan	100	12.68	25.36
Norway	36	18.63	25.34
Italy	50	13.20	19.80
France	50–60	12.75	19.76
United States	36	14.31	19.46
Spain†	63	8.81	14.36
United Kingdom	33	10.48	13.94
Taiwan	30–60	3.43	4.97
Hong Kong	20	2.85	3.42
Brazil†	80	1.50	2.70
Mexico††	30–40	1.57	2.12

† 1988 figure.
†† 1987 figure.
Source: World Business Reports, Ernst & Young International, and U.S. Department of Labor

The following are some general overviews of industrial relations in different regions of the world. Please keep in mind that these are generalities and may not hold true in every case. However, the reader will gain an idea of what it is like to do business in these areas relative to hiring locals.

Europe

In Europe, the government plays the biggest part in setting benefits. Quite often, the government dictates the statutory work week and overtime, sets salaries, and makes requirements in the work environment. The government's strong leadership role leads to

- Decreased productivity;
- Equalization of the work environment; and
- Greater job security for employees.

Job security reduces employee turnover and seems to enhance employee loyalty. However, low turnover may be due to high severance costs.

Following are highlights of some of the benefits typically provided in West Germany, to give you an example of European benefit requirements.

Benefits Overview—West Germany

- *Sick pay.* Employer must pay full salary for six weeks, after which salary is paid by insurance.
- *Maternity leave.* Mother has employer-paid leave six weeks prior to birth and eight weeks after birth. Health insurance will pay for eight months after this, after which time the employee is obliged to resume employment.
- *Company pensions.* Voluntary company pensions supplement state pension plans.
- *Bonuses.* One month to one and a half month's salary paid in two installments.
- *Paid leave.* Average six weeks vacation and ten to thirteen legal holidays.

Asia

In Asia, a patriarchal attitude is often seen in the employer/employee relationship. The work atmosphere, or culture, is very family oriented and may be best defined as a benevolent dictatorship. The owner of the company in Malaysia, for example, is often called "the gadji payer" and takes the attitude of a parent to children. Many social benefits are left to the discretion of the employer, who feels it is his responsibility to take care of the employees.

In Asia, there are also relatively few unions and, in general, there appears to be a high degree of loyalty exhibited by employees to their employer as a result of the family-like atmosphere. An example of government-mandated benefits is shown below.

Benefits Overview—Malaysia

- *Sick pay.* Fourteen days for under two years employment; eighteen days for two to five years and twenty-two days after five years service. This is extended to sixty days for hospitalization.

- *Maternity leave.* Generally, mothers are given sixty days of paid maternity leave at a minimum of $1.60/day, with an optional ninety days unpaid.

- *Company pensions.* Employee's Provident Fund pays retirement benefits starting at age fifty-five. Contributions amount to 20 percent of employee's total wages (employer pays 11 percent, employee 20 percent). Some companies have their own plans to supplement this.

- *Bonuses.* Not compulsory but typically provided in the amount of one to two month's salary.

- *Paid leave (vacation).* Minimum eight days by law. Typically twelve to sixteen days.

Keep in mind that these are minimums and are often exceeded by the paternalistic owner of the company.

United States

There seems to be an impersonal attitude of companies towards employees and vice versa in the United States. Unions play a larger role in setting benefits, safety requirements and wages through negotiations than in many countries but only fifteen percent of the work force is represented by a union.

The question of employee benefits has become so politically

charged that the next few years may see a revival of unions and increasing government involvement. Union and government intervention may be necessary to create a work force of people who develop institutional knowledge within a company and apply their knowledge to keep our competitive edge sharp. Otherwise, the United States will have a work force of drifters, moving from company to company.

Benefits Overview—United States

- *Sick pay.* Hospital, medical, and surgical are not required by law. Typically, there is co-insurance with employee and employer contributions.

- *Maternity leave.* Left to the discretion of the individual employer.

- *Company pensions.* Social Security is usually supplemented by company-paid pension plans. The company pays 5 to 12 percent of the payroll annually depending upon the type of pension program, employee's age and length of service.

- *Bonuses.* Not an important part of compensation except for sales and executive personnel.

- *Paid leave.* This is not mandatory but generally employees receive one to two weeks at first, gradually increasing to four weeks.

As you can see, the United States requires fewer benefits than other regions of the world. The cost of additional benefits needs to be carefully evaluated when considering overseas operations or hiring. Benefits costs can be very significant compared to per capita income. Close attention to local salary and benefit costs is mandatory before making decisions regarding hiring of local staff or setting up foreign operations.

SPECIAL TIPS FOR SUCCESS OVERSEAS

Beating competitors at their own game is most often the result of long-term, systematic planning of the sort sketched in this book. Heeding the miscellaneous tips we are about to offer can give you an extra edge. These tips supplement the planning methods already described, and can help you identify potential problems before they arise.

Tip 1: Take sufficient time to select distribution channels carefully.

One of the most bizarre and least explicable tendencies of American business people going international is the impulse to set up distribution channels with little or no forethought. A high-level manager goes overseas for a week, talks with a few people, and quickly picks someone to represent the company. Later, this representative turns out to be disreputable or unreliable. The company is then stuck with a bad partner, bad operations, and a bad overall experience. All this can occur despite extensive experience in the domestic market.

Throughout the world it is possible to find first-rate business people who would make good partners. But finding these people takes a cautious search, because unfortunately, no country on earth suffers a shortage of incompetents, mediocrities, and scoundrels. Some potential representatives make false claims about their backgrounds or intentions. Others present you with falsified or unaudited financial statements. If you assume that such potential partners are honest and their companies are healthy, and if you commit yourself too fast, the facts will emerge eventually—and painfully.

To avoid problems of this sort, you should check every potential partner as thoroughly as (if not more so than) you would in the United States. At the very least, you should

- Investigate the firm's board of directors,
- Check all references,
- Determine if the representative has the staff he claims to have, and
- Verify that he has in fact acquired the contracts he claims to have.

Would you arrange a partnership in the United States without verifying your potential partner's background? Of course not. Yet many American firms close deals with overseas partners they scarcely know.

Ultimately, the question is the other person's integrity, qualifications, and reliability. You have to be hard-nosed. And to be effectively hard-nosed, you have to spend some time getting to know your potential partner.

Tip 2: When working with foreign representatives, grant them only as large a territory as they can cover effectively.

If your intention is to hire a representative to distribute your product overseas, you will probably find many people in any given country eager to work with you. However, some of these people may be unrealistic about how much territory they can cover effectively. They may request the rights to represent you in more than one country, and, perhaps even throughout an entire region. Unfortunately, few companies have a staff sufficient for such wide-scale operations. (For instance, the rights for all of Asia would involve a market of two and a half *billion* people.)

The reasons for this lack of realism among potential representatives are varied. Some reps simply don't know their own limitations. They may purchase the rights for a large territory only to discover that they can't sell your product effectively. Others know their shortcomings yet still bargain for extensive territory. Either way, granting excessive rights can put you in a bind.

For example, suppose you have a franchise operation. You sell the rights for Asia for $500,000 to a company that ultimately proves incapable of handling the entire region. This company then sells the rights *for each individual country in Asia,* except for the rights for Hong Kong, and earns a total of $750,000. The company then turns around and pays you $500,000. Without having paid a dime for the franchise, the original representative has gained a profit of $250,000 and has retained a particularly promising Asian market. Meanwhile, you end up in a position of having no information about or control over the people representing your products elsewhere in Asia. Risky? Of course. Yet this sequence of events takes place time after time.

Given these risks, you should sell the rights to your product *only to someone capable of handling the designated terrain.* If necessary, you should limit the terrain outright. Alternatively, you might consider offering initial rights for a particular country, with rights for further countries or regions open for negotiation when the rep proves his ability to handle the first country to your satisfaction. One way of showing your good faith is to offer the rep rights of first refusal on other territories. But in any case the rep must prove himself.

The exception to this rule is, of course, an arrangement with a big, well-established trading organization. Under these circumstances, you may not be able to call the shots. You may, in fact, not need to: such trading companies may present fewer problems in the first place. But even under these conditions you should look at the size of the company in relation to the territory the rep wants to acquire.

Other considerations are

- The number of people on the representative's staff,
- The number of products represented,
- The overall track record, and
- The representative's corporate history.

Tip 3: Grant representation rights for the shortest time possible.

Even when you find a representative who seems capable and realistic about his plans for your product, make sure you grant the rights for the shortest possible time under the circumstances. Many reps would like to have a long-range contract, sometimes covering a term of twenty years or more. You should negotiate a more limited term instead. Suggest, for example, that you will initially grant the rep rights for a year. At the. one-year point, you will review the situation and decide whether to continue or not. Such arrangements allow both you and the rep a chance to proceed or to withdraw, as necessary.

Understandably, many representatives will protest these terms. They are, after all, making an investment in representing you—both in terms of training and effort—and may therefore consider a brief term unfair. Such protests are not necessarily groundless. A year may in fact be too short a time, given the representative's own investment. If the rep does protest, you should attempt to negotiate an intermediate period—perhaps a three- to five-year contract, with an opportunity to review progress at the end of that period. If you can arrange something shorter, so much the better. A two-year contract is fine. A three- to five-year contract is fair. Anything beyond that, however, can be dangerous.

Tip 4: Tie a continuing relationship to the representative's performance.

This tip provides a useful escape hatch for the situations discussed in tips 1 and 2. During negotiations, offer the potential representative a three- to five-year contract *contingent upon his achieving a designated level of sales.* If his performance falls short of what you have agreed upon, then you have the right to terminate the contract with sixty days' notice. The agreement therefore includes concrete terms: the rep must meet certain sales goals. You set reasonable quotas; in turn the rep must meet them to continue the relationship.

Many smaller or medium-sized agents will agree to these terms. Larger firms balk at them or refuse them entirely. If your product is particularly promising, however—such as some high-tech or otherwise innovative products—you may be able to set some of the terms even if your company is relatively small and unknown.

Tip 5: Review performance at least quarterly.

Ideally, you should have your own manager on the scene to review overseas performance. If an on-site manager is not feasible, then you should make sure that someone from headquarters visits the field at least once per quarter. Less frequent reviews will prevent you from realistically seeing, feeling, and understanding the foreign market.

Information for review should come from

- firsthand observation by an on-site expatriate manager or manager from headquarters visiting the field,
- monthly reports from your agents or distributors overseas, and
- direct feedback during visits with overseas customers.

Less direct and abundant information may prove insufficient or misleading. It may even prevent you from perceiving accurately whether customers are truly satisfied with your products, service, response to their requests for orders, and so forth.

Moreover, on-site observation will allow you to understand the situation in ways that would be impossible from a more remote vantage point. Have you turned your product over to someone who represents it inaccurately or insufficiently? Is the rep promising that the product can do things that it can't, or promising that the company will introduce a new version shortly (when in fact you aren't planning that at all)? Is sales support adequate? The only reliable way to answer these questions is to go out and talk with your customers. In addition, your on-site presence or quarterly visits keep your agents on their toes. They know that you will not be simply reading their reports, but will be on their own turf interviewing clients yourself.

Tip 6: Assume that communications will be different from—and perhaps more difficult than—in the United States.

In a world where all countries are increasingly interconnected by electronic communication systems, it's tempting to assume that exchanging data is as easy overseas as within the domestic arena. The truth is certainly more complex.

Communicating in the global marketplace continues to present a variety of difficulties. Some of the problems are technical. Other problems result from time differences. Some of the most significant problems are cultural. When these various difficulties compound each other, the likelihood of trouble increases exponentially.

However frustrating they may be, technical and time issues are often relatively simple to work around. Cultural issues, by contrast, can be difficult to work around but dangerously easy to ignore. The cultural aspects of communications cause some of the biggest and most frequent headaches in overseas ventures.

For example, when you give orders by phone to multilingual host-country employees and reps who speak English as a second or third language, there may be misunderstandings and ambiguities. Moreover, people in different cultures perceive telephone communication in varying ways. Not all business people use the phone in the same way (or for the same purposes) as Americans do. Generally speaking, phone exchanges aren't considered quite as definitive as in-person conversations. In some countries, the government taps telephones; people therefore communicate less openly by phone. And in many cultures, people simply don't feel as comfortable with the phone, but prefer to meet face-to-face instead.

For these reasons, you should be aware of how communications may differ between the United States and your overseas location, and you should respond accordingly. In general, you should:

- Stay alert to cultural differences in communication styles, even when the hardware in use makes interaction seem universal;

- Back up conversations with a telex or FAX when it seems advisable; and

- Above all, do not believe that a telephone conversation can substitute for an on-site presence or frequent visits.

Tip 7: Make as few changes as possible to your product.

Frequently, overseas representatives will ask you to modify your product to suit their real or imagined needs. These requests are often well-intentioned and helpful. However, you should make sure that all modifications are realistic, and that the market is large enough to justify the trouble and expense of making them.

The ideal way to change your product is to make it adaptable to a variety of different circumstances. Japanese electronics firms, for instance, provide switches on many electronic appliances to convert the appliance from 110 to 120, 220, or 240 volts, as needed. Many companies also provide purchasers with a box of adapters that enable the appliance to fit various kinds of outlets in different countries. Their instruction booklets come in multiple languages. As a result, these firms can ship their products to a wide range of countries without having to make modifications for each market.

The worst method, in contrast, is to modify the product repeatedly and unsystematically, ending up with a German version, a French version, a Japanese version, a Taiwanese version, and so forth.

To proceed in the most effective and least disruptive way, you should accumulate a list of the whole range of potential modifications, decide which are realistic and which are unrealistic, and then determine how to combine as many of them as possible. The ultimate goal should be to make the fewest and most minimal changes possible. Ideally, you will end up with one universal version of each of your products. The next-best case would be one version for Europe, one version for Asia, and so on. By all means stay sensitive to any special local requirements. But keep in mind that your product simply may not be suitable for every country because of unusual or expensive requirements. Otherwise you will end up with a different product, a different inventory, different sales support service, and a different training program for each country, you have targeted. Making profits under those circumstances will be difficult—if not virtually out of the question.

Tip 8: Avoid the temptation to take shortcuts.

Throughout this book, I have emphasized the need for staying patient while going international. At the risk of harping on the subject, I must stress this point once again. An appalling number of American business people spend vast amounts of money and time preparing for an international venture, then ruin their chances of success by making hasty moves.

You *must* invest in training. You *must* monitor the results. You *must* guide your representatives and on-site expatriate staff through the initial phases of operation. And you *must* make periodic visits to interview some of your customers in person. Taking the time to learn about the host-country culture, getting to know your representatives before you commit to them, checking their background, having your local personnel visit headquarters—all these efforts will pay off in the long run. Simply tossing your product out like a message in a bottle and hoping it ends up somewhere worthwhile is a guaranteed route to failure.

Export trading companies—discussed in Step 1—are admittedly an inexpensive way to get started. However, using them at length, or without restrictive terms, often means you forfeit your control over a given territory in exchange for avoiding the risks of setting up your own operations. Export trading companies are a valid way to proceed, but at a high price.

There are no cheap shortcuts when doing business abroad.

Case Study

Jet Spray Corporation, a Massachusetts-based company with 400 employees, realizes more than 50 percent of its total sales from exports. The company has branches in Britain and Canada, and distribution in 100 countries. The company has been selling its beverage dispensers abroad since 1957.

In the early 1980s, the company lost much of its European sales to foreign competitors. In 1988, the company developed a Euro-

> ## Case Study (Continued)
>
> pean strategy, and sent marketing officials to every country within Europe in a four-month period. The company began to second source parts for its machines in Italy and is considering expanding its London operation to include assembly. This allows for better after-sales service. As a result of these efforts, the company realized a high growth of sales to Europe.
>
> The company has used foreign-language sales literature, operating instructions, and service manuals. In those countries where it does not develop local sales materials, the company provides pre-printed literature that can be translated and printed locally.
>
> The company makes a strong effort to recruit business school graduates with language skills. This enables it to communicate not only with distributors worldwide but also with their local customers.
>
> An interesting example of the company's flexibility occurred when a Dutch customer requested that their hot chocolate dispenser be produced using stainless steel, as opposed to the wood and plastic that was currently being used. Within a few weeks, to the amazement of the Dutch customer, Jet Spray prepared a prototype machine. As Jet Spray's international marketing and sales director said, "You can't imagine how surprised and pleased that man was" (*Journal of Commerce*, October 30, 1989).

Tip 9: Expect the pace of business to be different overseas.

In a few places—Hong Kong is a good example—the American pace of business is too slow. In most other places, however, it's far too fast. We Americans tend to arrive on foreign soil almost literally like invading commandos.

Time is different overseas. The American cliché that time is money strikes people in many cultures as offensive, even foolish. Time is time. Money is money. Time provides the opportunity to do many things, among them making money. But to equate time with money seems the height of arrogance and boorishness. Throughout most of the world, even the people most intent on making money see their business dealings in a wider, often complex context of relationships,

social obligations, regional and local customs, even religious obser-
vances, many of which affect the sense of time. To succeed in doing
business abroad, you should recognize these differences in time
sense and honor them to the greatest degree possible.

Especially in Latin America and Asia, the pace and sequence of
events differs dramatically from what seems familiar and sensible in
the United States. Europe has its own variations: some countries—
such as Germany and Switzerland—move a little faster, while
others—such as France, Italy, and Spain—move at a more leisurely
pace. Whatever else, business people overseas are more likely than
Americans to want to get to know you before proceeding with major
deals.

The crux of the matter is that *you can't do things overseas the way you
do them at home*. Don't get frustrated by the speed at which things get
done. The slower pace does *not* mean that your host-country partners and customers are uninterested in doing business with you.
Rather, they just have different priorities and a different style.

AVOIDING COMMON PITFALLS

Finally, there are seven pitfalls that trap U.S. companies need-
lessly but often. You should keep these pitfalls in mind throughout the course of beating your competitors at their own game.
The likelihood of encountering any particular threat is, of course,
uncertain. The risks vary from industry to industry and from
country to country.

Pitfall 1: Using Joint Venture Partners from the Start

Since many countries require local participation in foreign businesses, you may feel tempted to start off with a joint venture partner.
After all, such a partner will already have built a business
infrastructure within the host country. This approach involves two
risks, however:

1.   Missing out on better terms for local participation; and
2.   Finding that an established company makes its own business
     its first priority.

Countries requiring local participation may allow you to bargain for a phase-in of whatever arrangement you reach, often over an extended period of time. Moreover, some governments rescind local participation requirements when foreign investments start to dwindle. Accepting such requirements at face value is therefore unwise. You may reach better terms by holding off initially. Starting your operations unilaterally gives you time to make the best possible arrangements with the host-country government. If you ultimately decide to go ahead with a joint venture, the early delays—plus the firsthand experience you will have gained in the field—will work to your advantage when you actually choose a partner.

The other potential problem is that leaping headlong into a joint venture lands you with a company whose infrastructure puts your firm at an immediate disadvantage. Some companies may, in fact, want little more than to take your ideas, products, or technology for their own use, offering little or nothing to you in return.

As illustrated in the following Case Study, you should arrange a joint venture as knowledgeably as possible. Allow yourself a long period of corporate courtship before agreeing to the terms; then factor in more time to reach the final commitment—if any. Ideally, you should go ahead with a joint venture only after several years of experience with local business practices and the consequent knowledge of who within the local business community can or cannot be trusted. Only then will you know enough about the host country markets and methods of operation to identify the specific strategic advantages of linking up with a local firm.

Case Study

An electronics company set up a joint venture with a long-established firm in Malaysia. The Malaysian partner turned against the U.S. company, however, and eventually pulled enough strings within the local government to have the Americans expelled from the country. The upshot was that the U.S. firm relinquished control of its technology and product knowledge. The partner also used this arrangement to pick up other lines from competitors once they had learned the market through the advice and training that the Americans provided.

Case Study

Local representatives sponsor Lactoso Foods, Inc., in many parts of the world. Some of these reps talked the parent company into heavy investments for training the local staff and financing initial product inventories. The company has no U.S.-based managers on location with the representatives, however; as a result, the company's products tend to be either poorly displayed or not displayed at all. In many stores, the products seem all but swamped by the abundance of various competitors' goods.

Top management back in the U.S. cannot understand why sales are so poor. Every time they visit the region, their products are prominently displayed alongside rival brands. Little do they know that the local merchants dust off and display the firm's products only when the international vice president for marketing comes into town.

Pitfall 2: Using Representatives without Your Staffer on the Scene

For similar reasons, you should be wary of arrangements in which local business people represent your company without field supervision. Otherwise representatives may become more of a hindrance than a help, as shown in the Lactoso Foods Case Study.

As with joint ventures, you should consider using representatives only after an initial (and perhaps extended) period of learning the ins and outs of the local market, and after developing a firsthand knowledge of potential representatives' standing within the host-country business community.

Pitfall 3: Not Adequately Checking Out the Tax Situation—and Not Getting Guarantees on It

All too often, U.S. companies identify a target market and base their decision to enter it on current tax practices, since management feels safe for the period of tax holiday granted by the local government. However, many countries change their tax laws periodically—

sometimes overnight. (Within the past few years both Malaysia and the People's Republic of China, for example, passed laws that added a 20 percent withholding tax at source on remittances made overseas for consultancy services.) For this reason, you should take these precautions:

- Double-check the overall host-country tax situation as fully as possible.

- Include caveats as a part of any incentive program that you arrange with the local government.

- Make sure that caveats include statements that any subsequent changes made in tax laws will affect previous agreements, or, alternatively, that any changes will involve a penalty accruing to the government.

Remember at all times that your company is in its best bargaining position *before* you break ground in the host country or establish yourself in any formal way. During these initial phases, the government will be more receptive to you overall and will be more conciliatory in granting tax and other incentives. Once your company has started operations and has made some initial investment, you will generally find the local government less receptive to any pleas for changes or improvements to the original agreement. Such inflexibility once the investment has begun is often called the "international *gotcha.*"

Pitfall 4: Uncritically Accepting the Comment, "It Isn't Done That Way Here"

Although many American business people have, in fact, tended to be insensitive to foreign business practices, some host-country business people may use the issue of cultural differences as a device for manipulating you. By all means keep your radar finely tuned to local customs and protocol. But don't take every assertion at face value. If someone tells you that a certain business practice simply isn't acceptable locally, double-check the facts as carefully as possible.

Many times the claim doesn't hold up under scrutiny. Ask other reliable sources their opinions. Also, ask every source for *specific*

Case Study

An American consultant reviewed cash management procedures for a large company in Europe. He wondered whether the company should ask for bids on banking services. In the course of interviewing twenty-five of the largest banks in the country, he heard from each contact that their organization would never entertain the notion of such an unprofessional way of developing banking relationships.

Nevertheless, the consultant recommended to his client that the company prepare a request for banking services and submit it to the banks for a response. Each of the banks responded with offers of banking services at more competitive rates than the client had received in the past. The winning bank even offered to open a branch in the client's own building, thus giving the company quicker recognition of foreign and local checks, plus a reduced rate on the long-term and working capital debt. The company ultimately saved more than $2 million a year on its cash management.

examples of where other companies have attempted to do what is supposedly unacceptable and have failed in their efforts.

In short, accepting at face value all comments on how to do business in a particular setting *may* be a mistake. Consider the possibilities. Ask around. Check with your local contacts. And under some conditions, go ahead and try out your alternative.

Pitfall 5: Not Developing a Fallback Position

As part of your overall strategy, you should identify a second target market as a fallback position just in case something goes wrong with your first choice. Many companies doing business in the Middle East, for example, use Athens, Greece, as a fallback. A variety of firms retreated to Greece from Iran and Libya as political problems developed in those countries; the result was that their regional operations could continue with relatively minor disruption.

Similarly, companies doing business in either Hong Kong or

Singapore—or, for that matter, companies doing business in Southeast Asia but headquartered in Hong Kong or Singapore—sometimes use the other nation as a fallback. This is especially true for companies in Hong Kong. With the People's Republic of China scheduled to take over governance of Hong Kong in 1997, Hong Kong is both a high-risk and high-opportunity location. Many companies are establishing headquarters there, poising themselves for intensive work with China. Under the circumstances, these firms would be wise to consider Singapore as an alternative headquarters, since tax or financial conditions may change unpredictably when the PRC takes over.

Pitfall 6: Starting Too Big

Many American companies succumb to a classic misconception: To succeed overseas, you must open a big plant with a cast of thousands. Here as in other aspects, impatience and grandiosity often lead to disaster. Slow initial sales disappoint the company's top executives, who, resenting low returns on high investment, close down the operation and permanently drop the idea of ever going international.

By contrast, more successful firms generally start off on a smaller scale. They build only as the market expands, with on-site staff gaining knowledge of the local culture and markets that makes growth steady and more reliable than the flash-in-the-pan approach.

One of the best ways to start up reliable, productive operations is the "one-plus-one" approach. In this approach, you station one of your best people in your target market. This person's first responsibility is to find one good local counterpart. That local counterpart then helps the American to understand the local environment, business practices, legal issues, and so forth. In short, one expatriate plus one local business person form a team to get business operations started. Only then—and only little by little—does your company build its presence overseas. This approach provides flexibility and reliability at a relatively low cost. It also allows the company to build for the future by training the local counterpart to take a leadership role in the long run.

An added advantage of this approach is that if the government requires local participation at a later date, the local counterpart will be the ideal candidate. Through stock options, training, a long-term personal relationship, and other incentives, you will have established many inducements for the local counterpart to feel primary allegiance to your company.

Pitfall 7: Losing Control

Many American companies lose control of their overseas operations through lack of prudence—specifically, through failure to imagine all the ways in which their competitors may act or react.

Some nations' lax laws concerning copyrights and trademarks also allow foreign manufacturers to copy products and to sell them at a fraction of the original's cost. American companies whose products have been pirated in this manner receive no compensation. For this reason, you should give special consideration to safeguarding your products in these countries. Even with weak copyright and trademark laws, you can find ways to protect your products. One software company, for example, asks every buyer to sign a noncopying agreement, enforceable in both the United States and the country of origin of the buyer.

THE COMMITMENT TO WINNING

Step 4 has addressed a wide range of issues—wider, perhaps, than the range of those addressed in the previous three steps. But if any

---

Case Study

TNT Tobacco Corporation decided to enter several Latin American markets. Upon doing so, however, management discovered that a major competitor had recently entered Latin America as well, and had *registered all the brand names for all major American tobacco companies*, including those for TNT. This preemptive move may have been unethical, but it turned out to be legal. TNT Tobacco could not use its own brand names in Latin America. Prudent strategizing would have saved TNT from severe legal and marketing headaches.

single statement encapsulates the variety of issues in question, it is this: *If you really want to beat your competitors at their own game, then you must select your personnel with utmost care, take them seriously, and give them resources to do the job right.*

Does this all go without saying? Perhaps. But perhaps not. Otherwise why would so many American companies select their expatriate staffers without much forethought? Why would too many firms treat their overseas personnel with a mixture of disdain and envy, as if they were tourists on a junket? Why would a regrettable number of corporations set up international ventures, only to expect their executives and agents to work with limited funds and unreasonably tight time frames? The sad fact is that U.S. businesses want to beat the competition without committing themselves to a degree that makes success possible.

But you can go about things differently. You can approach your competition as if in a game of chess. You can move carefully and wisely. You can wait patiently.

And you can win the complex, challenging, often profitable game of going international.

PART 3

SUCCESS CAN BE YOURS

Going international is rarely easy; on the contrary, it requires clear thinking, careful planning, strenuous effort, and durable patience. Going international is not risk-free; it is usually expensive, complex, and unpredictable. Yet going international is often eminently worthwhile. In an age of economic interdependence, global communication, and heightened cultural interaction, many U.S. companies already feel a growing need to see not just the United States, but the entire world, as their marketplace.

The Ernst & Young Guide to Expanding in the Global Market has attempted to provide an overview of the process of going international. No single book can address all the issues relevant to such an intricate subject; however, my hope is that this book has provided an outline and sourcebook to help your company master the necessary tasks as you take your products or services to customers in other countries. As mentioned throughout the text, the *The Ernst & Young*

Resource Guide to Global Markets, 1991 offer additional leads to information, guidance, and funding.

Is going international worth the time, money, and effort required? There is, of course, no single answer to that question. Your company's goals, products, and financial circumstances are the biggest variables affecting the outcome. But the current trend is unquestionably for U.S. companies to consider the option of international ventures, and the trend is there for good reasons.

Perhaps the most convincing evidence that going international can be worthwhile is the experience of companies that have done so successfully. We therefore conclude by hearing what imaginative corporate officers in three small or medium-sized companies have done to expand their operations into overseas markets. Their experiences are good examples of how going international can be manageable, profitable, and even enjoyable.

PATTON ELECTRIC COMPANY, INC.

At a recent National Hardware Show in Chicago, a Taiwanese distributor approached Patton Electric Company's booth and expressed interest in representing the firm's products in his country. Patton Electric, a manufacturer of small appliances, had previously sold its products almost entirely within the United States. But gradually an international contract took shape.

"This gentleman represented a group of Taiwanese retail department stores," according to William Hunt III, Patton's vice president for sales and marketing. "He inquired about our heaters and became quite intrigued with the quality, design, and features of our products. After our initial discussion, we had further conversations, and as a result of our negotiations we received letters of credit for two large forty-foot shipping containers to be filled with seven thousand portable electric heaters bound for Taiwan."

This sale was a coup in more ways than one. Selling seven thousand units was, of course, a worthwhile sale for the company in its own right. But selling these appliances to the Taiwanese seemed surprising, since most portable electric heater fans available in the United States are in fact *made* in Taiwan. William Hunt says, "This is unusual. We haven't found any manufacturer of portable electric appliances who's shipping *any* electric appliances to Taiwan. Our sale is a first, as far as we've been able to determine."

Moreover, the sale has marked a change of direction for Patton Electric. Hunt notes that until recently, the company has focused almost entirely on the U.S. domestic market. However, recent changes in currency exchange rates have prompted executives at Patton to reconsider their marketing strategies. "Opportunities are just now beginning to open up," he explains, "due to the devaluation of the dollar. This makes our products more attractive. For many years, there was a demand for American-made products because of the worldwide perception that they are more modern, up-to-date, and of a little higher quality. They've been a kind of status symbol. But the problem has been that American products have always been too expensive. Now we are starting to see the trade situation change a little. We're getting new opportunities for export."

In addition, Patton has had to deal with a variety of engineering issues, issues that now seem worth addressing. "The biggest problem for Patton is not so much the problem of the dollar; it's the problem of electrical systems," according to William Hunt. "Different countries have different kinds of electrical systems, and they require different voltages and use different types and speeds of motors. These countries also have different types of electrical commissions and governmental authorities. So there's quite an array of constraints to selling electrical appliances. The technical types of problems that we are working to overcome can't be solved overnight just because the dollar drops."

The result is therefore not so much that Patton Electric anticipates a quick fix to these technical issues, but rather that the company now finds an incentive to deal with them over the long haul. "We are actually allocating resources to engineering projects designed to configure our products to work in 220-volt markets. The 220-volt market is, after all, the largest market in terms of the world's population. And the motors, of course, have to be 50 cycles instead of the 60-cycle motors we have in the U.S."

Modifying its products in these ways, Patton Electric intends to move carefully into overseas markets. "Since the time of our business expansion into Taiwan," Hunt explains, "we have been shipping merchandise into Mexico. Mexico has a similar current to ours. At the same time, we're having a representative attend the Domotechnica Trade Show in Cologne, West Germany, where we hope to attract new interest in our 220-volt configurations. We are also working on a joint venture for producing components in China, and we're working with the Chinese government to produce products for consumption inside of China."

Hunt summarizes how Patton has experienced going international. "Quite frankly, in this business you pretty much respond to a window of opportunity, but you respond in a way that's greater than just to that one window. When you have responded to that window, you say, 'Okay, let's see if we can enter other windows along the same line.' But there are a lot of unknowns. No one just instantly knows about all the barriers and restraints to trade in every country in the world. You have to investigate the most promising areas of opportunity, then develop the product, the design, and the means for moving the product into that country, and for selling it through."

What advice would William Hunt offer to other companies taking their products overseas for the first time?

"First of all, answer all requests. So many foreigners request information and send inquiries to U.S. manufacturers, but hardly any of them are ever answered. Even if your answer is, 'We can't do it,' or 'We can't do it right now, but maybe later'—always answer the request.

"Second, when someone shows an interest in your product or company, follow up. Even if they don't speak English, or if their ways are different, take the time to follow up. Because you have everything to gain and nothing to lose.

"Third, learn a little about your customers' country and their customs. So many times, we accidentally insult people because we don't take time to learn the simplest things about their culture. Our Taiwanese customers were fluent in English. Their trading representative had a U.S. office, so he spoke good English. But you're dealing with issues of politeness, respect, and care and understanding. This is how international trade is done. It's not the same as how many people do business in the United States with U.S. companies. You shouldn't come on too strong."

Patton Electric has found its international ventures challenging, requiring new plans, new ideas, and new ways of doing business; but the experience has also been a source of tremendous satisfaction throughout the whole company.

"In manufacturing those heater fans for Taiwan, I sensed a great sense of pleasure in the general work force of our company. There was a sense of pride for our workers in our plants. In fact, when they filled the last container with Patton heater fans, they actually went out and made a big sign that said, 'Proudly Made in the U.S.A. for the People of Taiwan.' And they put that sign in the container with the heater fans."

KATHY MULLER TALENT AND MODELING AGENCY

While in high school and college, Kathy Muller worked as a model and actress in Hawaii and California. Later, following a stint with an advertising firm in San Francisco, she founded the Kathy Muller Talent and Modeling Agency in her native Honolulu. Her company is now the largest theatrical, commercial, and modeling agency in Hawaii.

"After I'd been in business about a year," Muller explains, "I took a trip to Tokyo for P.R. purposes. From that point on, clients heard that we had quality models with the right look for Japan—and business just started exploding. The basis of my business became the Japanese market. Perhaps 65 percent of our revenue still comes from Japanese clients."

What sorts of arrangements has she made with these clients?

"We work with agencies that are already established in Tokyo and have a good track record. On my trips to Tokyo, I meet with the staff, take a look at their financial backing, make sure that their apartments are in safe areas, and see that everything is set up properly for our models. Then we rotate our models into the individual agency. They pay us a mother-agency commission—in other words, they pull a 20 percent commission, and they send either 5 percent or 10 percent back to us, depending on the model."

Muller goes on to explain that "the *hapa-haole* models—half-Caucasian, half-Japanese—are our management stars in the Japanese market. They are the girls who will get a one-year exclusive contract for $10,000 to $20,000, plus the shoot rate. That special half-half look is what the Japanese like. That is a major part of the Japanese market for us. We also book many Caucasian fashion models into Japan to make the whole package profitable for us."

More recently, Muller has expanded operations to send models to countries other than Japan. "We realized that in order to grow—to take the next step—we had to work with other markets in other parts of the world. About five years ago, we set up our international division and started sending models to Australia, Hong Kong, and most major agencies in Europe. So we now have Japanese clients who come to work with our models here in Hawaii; we have our models who go to Japan and rotate in for a two-month modeling stint with the agencies in Tokyo; and we have Caucasian-European models who head off to Australia, Paris, London, Milan, Munich, Hamburg, and Switzerland. A few years ago, we also added Spain to our circuit."

Muller plans other expansions of overseas work. "We're just starting to get our models into Hong Kong. The Hong Kong economy is very strong, and European-Caucasian models are very popular there. We're opening that area up this year. We have not tapped the Scandinavian countries yet, but that will be our next step, along with Taiwan and Korea."

Kathy Muller has obviously done well overseas. In just eleven years, she has not only succeeded beyond her own expectations; she has also helped to make Hawaii one of the major centers for modeling in the world. How does she explain her success in the global marketplace?

"Each country has its own personality that you have to adjust to," Muller says. "Going into Tokyo, I took a while to understand what they were looking for. I had to research the 'look' they were interested in. I developed an eye for the type of face they wanted—small and delicate, with some of the Japanese characteristics, yet with some Caucasian characteristics, too. Basically, you need to go into each area and find out what the need is, and then try to find that in your own community and supply it."

Cultural issues are also paramount. "With the Japanese, you have to learn to be patient. The way they do business takes more time than doing business in the U.S. You often sit down and enjoy the tea ceremony before discussing business. Americans are so used to rushing in, putting the papers on the table, completing the deal, and moving on to the next project. I've learned so much from the Japanese. Loyalty is important, and once they trust you, they trust you forever. They will never go around you once you set up that relationship. Business is done on a much more personal and structured basis."

She goes on to say, "We have a lot of companies in this country, that fizzled because they didn't take the time to visit their international market; they didn't go and meet people face to face. It's imperative that you do that. You can't carry on a business relationship just by mail. Your clients need to know the person they're working with. Internationally, that's a very important point—*the personal connection.*"

The Kathy Muller Talent and Modeling Agency now brings in about $1 million annually in revenues. Muller has expanded the business from an out-of-the-home operation to a multifaceted company representing approximately one thousand models and actors. She sees no immediate limits to her endeavors. "To run this sort of business," she concludes, "you should look around and see what the needs are. If people ask, 'Can you get me this or that?' then you say, 'Yes,' hang up the phone, and go get it. Every time a door has opened, we've just walked through it."

REECE CORPORATION

Reece Corporation, based in Waltham, Massachusetts, is a producer of machinery for the garment industry. While the company has been selling its products internationally for nearly 100 years, it was in the early 1980s that the company realized the time had come to make international sales its chief priority.

In late 1983, Peter J. Abate joined the corporation as its President and CEO. Abate had over 30 years of experience with the international division of Singer Company. Abate quickly refocused the company's resources to exploit the growing international markets for Reece's products.

Abate realized that the U.S. apparel industry was rapidly disappearing as more and more production of apparel went offshore. He recognized that Reece had a choice: to either continue to focus its efforts on supplying its remaining American clients, or to follow the industry to the countries where it was now producing. "In other words...," as Abate put it, "instead of developing new machines to boost sales in a slowing market, Reece began to develop strategies to penetrate the growth markets in the global garment industry."

At this point Reece was involved internationally. It had sales and service subsidiaries in Canada, France, Hong Kong, and West Germany, and a branch office in the United Kingdom. Approximately sixty independent agents worldwide represented and serviced its products. However, according to Abate, "This extensive organization was being driven by the idea that what was good for the U.S. market was good for the rest of the world."

Under the direction of Abate, the company undertook a restructuring of its activities. Responding to the challenge of the international market became a priority for the company. Changes were made in marketing focus as well as product and production. The company knew they had to produce a "very competitively priced and technologically competitive product line." And the result was success. In 1984, 41 percent of the company's revenues came from international markets. By 1987, this figure was 57 percent. As Abate stated, on reflecting upon this success.

> We know that we must have presence in growth countries. This is the only way to survive—and grow ourselves. We have a knowledge of our customer countries as a result of our network's research. We know, for instance, that Soviet businesses prefer a French or a British way of doing business. The Chinese, however, prefer an American style. We realize that Reece can not force its strategies on the consumer country. That's the key for Reece—for any business is to recognize your marketplace and know how it wants and likes to be served.

Reece's revenues increased from $40.3 million in 1983 to $57 million in 1987. It can readily be seen that most of this growth was from international sales. Reece realized the opportunities of foreign markets, and seized upon them. (*Northeast International Business*, November 1988, pages 11–12.)

OTHER SUCCESS STORES

The above-mentioned companies are just a few examples of the many small and medium size companies that have achieved success in international markets. You do not have to be a Fortune 100 company to be successful in the international marketplace. A recent survey by the American Business Conference showed that medium-sized companies (between $25 million and $1 billion in sales) recorded strong growth in overseas sales, exports, and operating profits from 1981–1986, when the overseas operations of many other companies were constricting. According to the ABC survey, these companies have also been achieving levels of overseas profitability equal to the high levels they earn in the United States. There are numerous other companies that have realized success, for example:

B&D Instruments of Valley Center, Kansas, a producer of aircraft products, exports approximately 25 percent of its total sales of between $10 and 15 million through 47 dealers in 27 countries.

Filament Fibers of Bay Head, New Jersey, a $20 million manufacturer of polypropylene fibers and other specialty materials, purchased a $5 million facility in France to ensure access to the European Community.

Checkpoint Systems of Thorofare, New Jersey, with sales of approximately $35 million, exports 25 percent of its total sales to Europe and has set a goal to increase overseas sales to 50 percent of its total sales.

Lancer Corporation of San Antonio, Texas, a $32 million producer of equipment for the soft drink industry followed its customer base of large U.S. soft-drink manufacturers overseas and now export 16 percent of its sales to 68 countries.

Nordson Company of West Lake, Ohio, an industrial equipment manufacturer with $250 million in sales, of which 30 percent are in Europe, sells in eight countries through a network of wholly-owned distributors, six servicing centers and four product adaptation centers.

Millipore Corporation, a producer of high-tech separation membranes for scientific and engineering uses, is headquartered in Bedford, Massachusetts. Fifty-eight percent of its $261 million in sales are from Europe, where Millipore has established a strong stable of subsidiaries after initially entering France in 1964.

The list goes on and could fill a book. When a U.S. company goes international and is successful, it is joining numerous other companies who have already paved the way. The techniques I have discussed above do work, and can lead your company to greater profits and to increasing challenges.

WANTED: THE ORIGINAL AMERICAN CAN-DO ATTITUDE

When I left the United States almost seventeen years ago to take my first overseas assignment, Americans routinely expressed pride in their country's products, services, and overall business practices. This pride was often entirely appropriate. U.S. businesses did, in fact, manufacture excellent products and provide first-rate services; and in response to such excellence, consumers throughout the world coveted and admired American goods and skills. Working among other expatriate Americans, I sensed confidence in our nation, our technology, and our future. Many expats would compliment a high-quality item or service in the host country by calling it "positively Stateside."

Upon returning home, however, I learned quickly that times had changed. Many Americans now criticize our own products, services, and business practices. It's common wisdom that U.S. goods are shoddy, our services are indifferent, and both our goods and our services cost far too much.

It goes without saying that American business people have learned a lot from our competitors in other countries. We aren't perfect, and we know it. Foreign competitors have created admirable innovations in technology, management, marketing, and other aspects of business. There's nothing wrong with learning from others' experience. However, the often blindly accepted clichés about American mediocrity are disturbing and, worse yet, counterproductive. The litany of complaints tends to become a self-fulfilling prophecy.

Since my return to the United States, I've made a point of buying U.S.-made products. I find little justification for the widespread complaints about their quality. Neither do I find that they are generally or disproportionately more expensive than their foreign-made equivalents. American service firms, meanwhile, offer a wide range of services that equal or exceed (and often far exceed) what I encountered overseas. So much for the decline of American craftsmanship.

What strikes me as truly unfortunate about this situation is that it need not have developed in the first place. To the extent that American products and services can be made better or sold cheaper than they are at present, we should pursue—both as individual executives and as a nation—the necessary means to increase U.S. excellence and competitiveness abroad. To the extent that our products and services are already good, we should grasp the reality of the situation, call a spade a spade, and stop running ourselves into the ground. The alternative to common sense in this regard is commercial decline. If we don't stop distorting the present, we stand no chance of facing the future with any chance of success.

Patton Electric Company, Inc., Kathy Muller Talent and Modeling Agency, and Reece Corporation are three examples of American companies that have accepted the challenge of doing business abroad. As success stories, these firms deserve admiration and emulation. Yet these three are only a few of the U.S. companies that produce excellent goods or services. Countless others have achieved their own levels of excellence. Still, as noted at the beginning of this book, only a small minority of American firms take their products and services overseas.

The fact remains: American companies can succeed in the global marketplace. They can earn profits, attain greater name recognition, and increase competitiveness at home as well as abroad. But success requires not only completing the tasks outlined in this book; success also depends on the original American can-do attitude.

Are you willing to take advantage of that global marketplace? Are you willing to take the risks and do the work? Are you willing to seek and find the opportunities awaiting you overseas?

Is there really an option?

PART FOUR

FINAL OBSERVATIONS AND THE CHALLENGES AHEAD

Many topics have been covered in the previous chapters. I have seen the process new-to-export companies must follow to become successful exporters. I have presented a method for experienced companies to improve their global position. Throughout it all, I have shown examples of companies which have ignored the fundamentals and failed, or have realized success through following the proven approach.

This final chapter will make some observations on what is termed the "export mentality" issue: how executives think about exporting, and how they respond to the challenges, fears, and uncertainties brought about by the new global market. Specifically, it will address the export mentality of American firms.

Since the first edition of this book three years ago, I have worked closely with nearly fifty companies, and have had substantive discussions with many more on a regular basis. There are a number of common issues which American business must address to be successful in the international marketplace.

UNREALISTIC EXPECTATIONS

One of the primary problems I have seen is that American business people have unrealistic expectations about what they can accomplish for the amount of time and effort they are willing to give.

American business people often try to accomplish too much too quickly. I have seen companies try to get into twelve European countries at the rate of three a month and fail miserably. I have also witnessed companies try to get into ten countries in three different regions simultaneously. Resources were stretched too thin to adequately understand the local markets, culture and regulations. Their efforts were doomed to fail.

American companies also expect things to occur at a pace they are used to in the United States. This is simply unrealistic and culturally biased. Most parts of the world do not share this "let's get right down to business" attitude. Business people in many cultures expect relationships to develop naturally between companies, and in some cases, friendships to be formed. In addition, many places of the world do not have the same sense of urgency that Americans do. Patience in international business is a key and necessary virtue. For some reason, Americans expect that minimum effort can yield great returns in international business. They expect more from international activities than domestic. This should be reversed, especially at the initial stages of going international or of opening a new market. I have seen too many business people take one trip to a country and expect a sale to be made. Or to locate distributors simply by looking at a few directories and sending off a bunch of letters and faxes. If anything, American businesses are going to have to put in extra effort to catch up with their competitors.

INDECISIVENESS

I have noticed that U.S. companies' indecisiveness has impeded their international business efforts. For example, many companies become excited about going overseas, or about expanding their present activities and then, within a period of six months, change their ideas and directions. They may refocus their attention to the domestic market, or switch their regions of interest in response to the nightly news. In the end, many of them become so confused they do make a decision—to do nothing.

I have also noticed that many U.S. companies may not make decisions during vacation periods such as August or between Thanksgiving and New Year. This seriously hinders international deal making. The countries with whom they are doing business may not be on the same vacation schedule.

Finally, U.S. companies are often not as decisive in responding to key opportunities for international trade. After the U.S.–Canada Free Trade Agreement was signed, our Canadian affiliate conducted a survey which found that over 60 percent of Canadian companies were planning to take advantage of the new agreement and enter the U.S. market. During the same period of time, not one U.S. company approached our International Trade Advisory Services group to discuss the Agreement. This is a scary example of how companies in other countries were reacting to changes while the United States was sitting back and not taking action.

Perhaps the source of this indecisiveness is that American business culture is risk-averse. Perhaps it's simply the lack of experience in dealing with foreign markets. Whatever the reasons, corrective action needs to be taken now so that the United States is not left further behind in the global marketplace.

AMBIVALENCE TOWARDS GOVERNMENT ASSISTANCE

As previously mentioned, there is a wealth of international business assistance available from both Federal and State agencies. U.S. companies seem to have an ambivalent attitude towards this assistance. This attitude is an obstacle to effectively using the assistance.

On one hand, companies have an attitude that government agencies are ineffective, that they cannot and do not provide useful services to "really help them with what they need." Government agencies are viewed as unwieldy bureaucracies lacking private sector sensibility. On the other hand, these same companies expect the government to be at their beck and call, to be able to assist them in all of their specific problems, and to solve the more general problem of the loss of American competitiveness. Neither of these attitudes is accurate and fair, nor are they constructive in the quest to develop a company's exports or to redress the American trade balance.

American business must come to a fair recognition of what services the government can provide and what they cannot do. Government agencies are usually large bureaucracies and have the inherent problems associated with all large organizations. On the other hand, many government employees are committed to do the best for their constituent companies. Once the realities and limitations of government services are known, companies can put these services to good use. The U.S. Department of Commerce, the Export Import Bank, the Overseas Private Investment Corp., and the State Export Development Agencies, among others, all can provide useful assistance to companies. The companies must firmly know, however, that it is up to them to do the job of selling their products overseas.

I am reminded of the case of a U.S. company that approached a government agency for a substantial amount of financial assistance. At the meeting the project officer tried to obtain pertinent information to take to his boss to argue why the government should back the project. The questions he asked were to the point; he was simply trying to obtain the basic financial and business structure of the proposed project. The company executives thought, however, that he was being negative. They began to wax philosophical about how the United States would lose the business to the Europeans or the Japanese if the U.S. Government did not support the project. The project officer politely listened to these comments, and tried to return to questions of direct relevance, which the executives took as his challenging them. The meeting finally ended, with the project officer committed to arguing for the project to his boss. The executives left the meeting, however, discouraged, thinking that there was no way they would get support.

The executives had unrealistic expectations about what the government could do for them and how fast they would act. Would they expect to go to a bank and receive a loan guarantee for $50 million without providing sufficient financial information?

LACK OF A CLEARLY DEFINED OBJECTIVE

One of the biggest problems I have found in assisting companies is that they have not established clear objectives based on why they want to go overseas and where they want to go. It appears that companies respond to the latest *fad* in international trade, rather than developing sound business strategies. The increased coverage of world events in general and of international trade in particular greatly contributes to this. One year companies read that China is the market to go to, so trips are taken to China, businesses established, executives enroll in Chinese language courses. Two years later, there is turmoil in China, but Eastern Europe presents new opportunities. Trips are taken, and the cycle begins all over. Companies must carefully develop their international business. They can use the techniques we have presented in this book, or perhaps other approaches. Whichever way is chosen, the important thing is to develop and focus attention on clear goals.

LACK OF SUPPORT FROM THE CEO

I discussed in an earlier chapter that one of the ten principal criteria for determining whether a company is ready to go overseas is the support of the CEO. We saw in another chapter that for the experienced company the commitment of management was a crucial influence on the company's in-house capabilities, and therefore on its global strategic position.

In many cases, the vice presidents of marketing and international, and even the chief financial officers, may fully believe they should proceed with international ventures. However, the CEO is not committed to take such an action. Without this commitment, the likelihood of success decreases dramatically.

Before a company undertakes an evaluation of whether or not to go international or decides to enhance its global position, it must get the explicit commitment of the CEO. If this is not there, all the market entry and expansion strategies, the proposals from consultants, and so forth, will result in nought.

I have shown a number of companies that there are significant markets for their products overseas, and helped them to develop strategies for accessing or expanding in these markets. In some cases, I learned that the strategies were not implemented for one simple reason: Ultimately, the CEO did not want to do more internationally in the first place. This taught me a valuable lesson: I will not work with companies on their international activities unless the CEO is actively involved in the entire process. This in a sense modifies one of the ten criteria. The CEO must not only demonstrate interest and commitment, in most cases he must play an integral part in global business development.

NOT TAKING THE PROBLEM SERIOUSLY ENOUGH

The final issue goes to the core of all the other issues. U.S. business simply does not take the problem seriously enough. The old American attitude of "everything will work out in the end" will not improve our trade deficit, will not improve American competitiveness, and will not expand your company's international sales.

THE CHALLENGES AHEAD

In spite of all of these problems, I am very optimistic about the prospects for U.S. international business. If not, I would not have spent the time writing this book. I have faith in the American business community and believe that they can expand in international markets, that our small, medium and large companies will respond to the challenge of the global market and succeed, and that our country will continue to grow and prosper.

In summary, I offer the following challenges to American business:

- *To commit the time and resources required* to expand their international markets and *to have the patience* necessary to realize the eventual gains from these actions.

- *To become decisive* in response to the reality of the global market-place.
- *Cooperation by industry and government* to increase America's competitive position. I call for American businesses *to have a realistic view* of what government can and should do to help them achieve their goals.
- *To develop clearly defined* objectives for international trade and not to follow spur of the moment ideas and fads.
- *For CEOs to demonstrate the commitment* necessary for their company to be a successful player in the global market.
- *To demonstrate that they will meet* the new realities of international competition seriously.

In conclusion, I would like to present the words of Dick Ayers, Chairman of The Stanley Works, a company that has been extremely successful in international business: "All American companies need to be sensitive that the world is shrinking in a trading sense. It is much easier for products from other parts of the world to come into what traditionally have been our markets. Whether a company has decided to go international or not, it needs to have that good understanding of its competitors from overseas as soon as possible in order to be a strong company and protect its domestic markets. My view is that the best way to understand that competition is to compete in those foreign markets."

INDEX

To receive your *free* year of *M&A Strategist*, complete the coupon by printing your name and complete address. Mail your coupon to:

John Wiley & Sons, Inc.
605 Third Avenue
New York, NY 10158-0012
Attn: Jeff Brown, *M&A Strategist*

Print Name _____ Date _____

Address_____

City _____ State _____ Zip _____

This coupon must accompany request. Offer expires January 1, 1992.